DELICIOUS MAURITIUS

DELICIOUS MAURITIUS

Tastes and Tales from my mother's kitchen

SONIA KAWALPUTTEE DURJUN
AND KEVIN DURJUN

For my Grandfather

Leaving Port Louis

What a view!!
Lights lighting up the ship,
The sky above and the sea below.
Magic!

Sonia Kawalputtee Durjun

Contents

Introduction — 1
The Big House — 3

Equipment — 5

Bread - Di Pain — 6
Nani's Naan — 7
Dal Puri — 9
Faratha — 13
Puri — 15
Bootiful Bread Rolls — 18

Party Snacks and Assorted Nibbles — 20
A Moonlit Mauritian Party — 21
Tiny Shop — 22
Gram — 23
Vegetable Samosas — 25
Variations on Samosas — 30
Fish Samosas — 31
Lamb Samosas — 33
Sega Dancing — 35
A Tale of Two Birdies — 36
Kaka Pison — 37
The Mystery Of The Floating Gateau Piment — 39
Gateau Piment — 40
A variation on Gateau Piment: Kurhi — 43

Gateaux Brinzels	46
Prawn Bhajia	50

Dips and Chutneys — 51

Coconut Chutney	52
Simple Coriander Chutney	54
Shrimp Chutney	55
Salt Fish Chutney	57
Mint Chutney	59
Roast Aubergine Chutney	60
Simple Tomato Chutney	62
Egg Chutney	64
Home Made Plain Yoghurt	65
Raita	67

Meat — 69

Tandoori Chicken	70
Lamb Curry	72
Lamb Daube	74
Chicken Curry	76
Vijay	78
Venison curry	79

Pickles — 81

Mango Koucha	82
Fish Vindaye	84
Vegetable Pickle	86
My Dad who Planted Trees	89
Pineapple with Salt and Chilli	90

Soups and Dals — 91

Bouillon	92

Black Dal	94
Dal Pitha	96
Channa Dal	98
Dynorod Soup	101
Crab Soup	104
Saffron	107
Fire	109

Seafood — 110

Gigantic Grilled King Prawns	111
Mauritian Fish Curry	114
Les Quatre Bandes	117
Prawn Curry	118
Sardine and Tomato Salad	120
Octopus Curry	121
Octopus Cooked in the Pickling Style	124
Din's Recipe for Octopus Curry	126

Rice — 129

Kitcheri	130
Chicken Biriyani	132
Vegetable Biriyani	137
Lamb Biriyani	141
Fish Biriyani	144
Mauritian Fried Rice	145
Vinaigrette Sauce for Fried Rice	148
Noodles with Chicken and Prawns	149
Easy Peasy Rice with Cumin and Cardamon	152
Chicken Risotto	154

Cakes and Sweets — 156

Manbogh	158
Khaja	160
Banana Loaf Cake	163
Mauritian Tea	165
Gulab Jamun	166
Jilabi	169
Besan Ludoo	172
Gateau Batat	174
Kheer	177
Tukmaria	179
Poa	181
Tekwa	183
Tekwa Dal	186
Corn Pudding	189
About my Dad's Mother	191
Napolitaines	192
Satwa	194
A Reflection on Mauritian Picnics	198
Cornettos in the car	199
La Laura	200
Semolina balls	201
Some Common Mauritian Phrases	203

Vegetables and Vegetarian Food   205

Schou Schou	206
A Vegetarian Feast: Pumpkin, Kutchoo and Channa Dal	208
Pumpkin	209
Kutchu	211
Simple Cabbage	213
Butterbeans in Light Tomato Broth	215

Butterbean Curry	217
Spicy Chickpeas	219
Bean Curry	221
The Blue Ford	224
Egg Curry	225
Easy Cook Ladies Fingers	227
Cauliflower, Potato and Pea Curry	229
Dodo	231
About the Authors	232

Introduction

At the height of the swinging 60s my mother swapped her embroidered saris for miniskirts and made the crossing from the small village of Long Mountain, Mauritius and moved to the urban streets of Tooting, South London. Her attire and beehive hairdo may have utterly changed but her healthy appetite for the food of her homeland remained steadfast. Every evening her tiny London kitchen would be filled with the sizzles, fragrance and flavours of Mauritius as she conjured up up a taste of home.

Delicious Mauritius is a celebration of traditional Mauritian cookery - and your open invitation to experience the unique cuisine of the island of Mauritius. The recipes featured in this book range from tea time cakes and street food snacks - quick and easy fodder for hungry schoolchildren, to elegant evening dishes that take time and planning to create and are perfectly suited for a special event. Best of all however, you will learn how to create the mouthwatering food that my mother grew up on, the food that was prepared for her by her very own mother.

I have thought about writing this book for over ten years. My mother and I only got around to writing it during last year's lockdown - clearly the idea needed plenty of time to marinade. The lockdown meant that we weren't able to be physically be close to each other for several months. So we spoke every day by video call. My mother dictated the recipes and I would try to keep up with her, typing away from my home just a few miles away.

I think that there is something fitting about us creating this book in this way. Even though we were apart we remained connected through food.

Kevin Durjun, October 2021

The Big House

Should you ever decide to travel to the village of Long Mountain, Mauritius keep going about half way up the Route Royale and you will come across The Big House. The Big House is a largish property set well back from the road with the curious honour of being the first two storey residence to have ever been built in Mauritius. For this reason many older Mauritians know of it - even to this day. The Big House happens to be where my mother grew up as it was built by her father for his family.

Although over time The Big House has become a little crumbled around the edges it still retains many vestiges of its former glory. Its generous gravel-filled in and out drive is today punctuated with the occasional bit of builder's rubble from more recent renovations. The drive wraps around a circular garden that is now neatly planted with row upon row of pineapples (I believe of the Victoria variety). Follow this and you will arrive at a few steps that will lead you up onto an expansive porch that wraps the whole front of the house. Cool white pillars lead your eye upwards to the bedrooms which are located upstairs on that famed second storey.

Go inside and you will walk over a glinting parquet of waxed ebony wood - the methodical application of the top of a coconut keeps it looking glossy. For those of you that want to give this a try you need to push the fibrous part across the floor using your foot and swish it from side to side - it takes quite some practice to do it right. The carpenter that fashioned that floor out of solid chunks of ebony one day carved my mother her very own rolling pin out of the very same wood.

A few steps behind the main house, surrounded by trees there was another smaller building - I suppose it was the kitchen. The smell of twigs, wood smoke and smouldering. A kettle boiling, an old woman - white hair, white sari. Milky sweet tea, more milk than tea.

Equipment

Here are some of the things that you will need to make the Mauritian recipes in this book. There is nothing particularly remarkable about any of the kit and and you will probably have most of the items already. If not, how lovely - you will get to go shopping!

- Large mixing bowl
- Pressure cooker
- Large heavy bottomed pot
- Weighing scales
- Rolling pin and board
- Spice grinder
- Pestle and mortar
- Measuring jug
- Blender
- Frying pan or flat plate
- Large wok
- Slotted spoon
- Pastry brush
- Fish slice (or heat-resistant asbestos fingers, like my mum has)

Bread - Di Pain

Mauritians adore bread. From plain bread rolls thickly buttered and filled with warm gateaux piment for breakfast, to soft flat breads such as faratha and puri that are torn and used to scoop up scrumptious slick and spicy curries, most Mauritian meals will feature some form of bread. They are easier to prepare than you might think - if my sister's children Harry and Miss Uma can roll out a dal puri then so can you!

- Nani's Naan
- Dal Puri
- Faratha
- Puri
- Bootiful Bread Rolls

Nani's Naan

Pronounced Nanny's Naaaaan

When my mum first became a grandmother everyone wondered what to call her. Nani was the name that stuck. Nanni's Naans are pillowy soft puffy breads that are incredibly easy to make and are my mum's own special recipe. Tear tiny bits off and use your dainty fingertips to pick up various morsels of your evening meal. These taste wonderful when they are served warm.

This recipe will make 5 naan.

Ingredients:

- 250 grams of white plain flour
- 2 tablespoonfuls of vegetable oil
- 3 tablespoonfuls of plain yoghurt
- 1 generous pinch of bicarbonate of soda
- 1 generous pinch of baking powder
- 8 tablespoonfuls of milk
- 1/4 teaspoonful of salt

Optional - 1 clove of garlic, crushed and finely chopped
Optional - 1 tiny bunch of coriander finely chopped

Method:

Put your flour in a mixing bowl. Drizzle this with your oil. Sprinkle with the bicarb, salt and baking powder and dollop in your yoghurt. Mix this all together for a few minutes until everything has mixed together well. Use your own fair hands to knead everything together and as if by magic it will transform into a stringy dough.

Now slowly add your milk, mixing it all together until all the milk has been absorbed. Gently knead your dough, don't be too heavy handed about things, and knead it in your bowl for 8 minutes precisely.

Let your dough rest for at least 1, preferably 2 hours, covered up with a plate. It doesn't need to go into the fridge, just on the side is fine.

Now, divide the dough into 5 balls.

Roll each one out into either a round shape (15 cm diameter) or into the shape of a rounded ciabatta (15 x 10cm). Try to not press the dough too hard or go too big otherwise your naan will not puff up as much. It will still taste nice though. Do this just before you are ready to cook each one or the dough might stick to your board.

Put your hot plate or frying pan to heat over a high heat. When it is hot it is time to cook.

Gently pick up your rolled dough and put it down flat to cook. Let it cook for 1 - 1½ minutes. You will notice bubbles coming to the surface. Using a fish slice, turn the naan over. Allow it to cook for another 1 - 1½ minutes on this side. The cooking naan will start to puff up. Brush one side of the naan with some oil, turn it over and brush again with oil. Turn it over occasionally. You will know that your naan is cooked when it turns a pale golden colour. Total cooking time for 1 naan is around 3 minutes.

Dal Puri

Pronounced Dal Pou-ree

Whenever we go to Mauritius a visit to a market to purchase fresh dal puris is a highlight of the holiday - one that is best enjoyed on as many occasions as possible. The dal puri seller will pick up a pair of warm dal puris, round and soft dal-filled flatbreads and will then fill them with with a splash of butterbean curry, a smear of hot chilli sauce and a smidgen of spicy chutney and roll it all up in a twist of paper. You need a pair as they are pretty delicate. You can eat 'em either hot or cold. We bought these once from a market in Saint Pierre, Mauritius. The chef recognised my dad as a childhood friend and refused to let him pay.

My mum proudly proclaims that this recipe will be suitable for vegans!

Serve this with:

- Daube of Lamb or Chicken (clearly *not* vegan)
- Aubergine Curry
- Tomato Chutney
- Butterbeans
- Khir (Mauritian style rice pudding)

This recipe will make around 25 dal puris

Ingredients:

- For the dough you will need

DELICIOUS MAURITIUS

- 1lb of plain flour
- A spoonful of oil (this will help to make your dal puris soft) vegetable or corn oil are fine
- A sprinkle of salt
- Half a teaspoonful of turmeric

For the filling:

- A cup full of channa dal or a cup full of dry chickpeas. My mum uses channa dal because her dad preferred it because he always had gas and thought that chickpeas might exacerbate the problem…
- A teaspoonful of cumin, toasted
- Half a teaspoonful of turmeric
- 1/2 a teaspoonful of salt

Method:

First you need to boil your channa dal (or chickpeas if you are the daring type) Put these to boil slowly slowly (my mum's words, not a misprint!) in about 3 - 4 cupfuls of water with a bit of salt in it. This will take about 1/2 hour. Don't cover it as it will boil over and make a big mess of your cooker. If it needs more water and it is not cooked, you can add some more to it. If you decide to use the chickpeas, cook these in exactly the same way.

After the channa dal is boiled and they have achieved a nice and soft consistency you drain the water away. Then you need to grind it.

My mum told me that when she was little, they would grind this outside in the garden using a very large stone. Here we don't have these sorts of things so you need to make use of whatever gadgets that you have. There is no benefit to grinding it by hand. Grind is grind according to my mum. Just make sure that no whole peas or large bits of dal remain. You can even use a blender to do this.

You now need to toast the cumin seeds in a frying pan. Dry fry them, do not use any oil for this. Fry them for about 2 minutes until you can smell the aroma which will be lovely. Then you need to grind these cumin seeds. It won't work if you try to do this in a wet blender, so don't use the blender that you have just used for the chickpeas. Instead use a pestle and mortar or take out a rolling pin and a board and crush them on that until they have become a powder.

Next leave everything to cool down. You could actually do the boiling and grinding the day before.

Now onto the dough.To make the dough you take your plain flour and add this to a large bowl. (My mum never sieved the flour in her entire life, but she has just told me to "Put sieve that flour" as she wants to be fancy) To this add a spoonful of cooking oil, your salt, your turmeric powder.

Make a well in the middle of all of these things and then add lukewarm water to make a soft dough. Mix it all together with your hands. It needs to be a manageable soft dough, not too sticky or runny. Afterwards you set it aside for half an hour.

Now you need to put everything together. Take a ping pong ball size of the dough in your hand. Make a hollow in the middle with your finger - enough to hold about a level tablespoonful of the ground chickpea mixture. Pull all of the dough together so that it resembles a pursed mouth and so that the chickpea mixture is contained right in the middle of the dough ball, and the dough ball is completely sealed. Put this aside onto a floured plate so that it doesn't stick. Repeat this until you have used up all of the dough and the filling. You will make about 25 of these.

Now, let's get rolling! Put some flour onto the board. Flatten the dough ball gently and them roll it out until it is about 5 inches in diameter. My mum boasts that she can roll her dal puris out to 7 inches, but this feat takes practice. It will be roughly 1 - 2 mm in depth. Once rolled out put onto a plate. As the uncooked dal puris will stick together if you stack them on top of each other keep them on separate plates. You will be able to cope with up to 5 dal puris at a time. After this point there will be too many plates!

Put a hot plate to heat on high. Or if you don't have one of these you can use a large frying pan. Carefully lift the rolled out dal puree from the plate. It is quite delicate at this stage so if you are a bit rough it might split, spilling all that lovely dal everywhere, so be gentle. Using your hands transfer the dal puri to the hot plate. Lower the heat to medium and let it cook for about 1 minute. You will notice that the dal puri turns a slightly darker colour and if you are particularly lucky it may also start to puff up.

Now brush the dal puri with a little oil, then using a fish slice turn it over. Brush the other side as well, let it cook for a little while, then take it out. In total the cooking time for 1 dal puri is about 2 minutes. Repeat until all of the dal puris are cooked in this way, stack them up one on top of another. If you feel the need to cover the stack of golden dal puris with a plate, desist - they will sweat if you do this. If you worry about them getting cold, then you can cover them with a tea towel.

Faratha

Pronounced Fa-rah-ta (this sounds like it could be a song from the Mauritian version of The Sound of Music doesn't it?)

Farathas are wholesome round soft breads, cooked on a hot plate, best served immediately. You can eat them in several ways - tear off bits and use them to scoop up bits of sauces and vegetables, or you can drizzle the whole lot with honey, roll them up and dip them in a big mug of creamy milk. This happens to be my favourite way of eating them.

We would always have Farathas on Mondays served with Bean Curry. When I was little I was never a big fan of Bean Curry. As a reward for finishing my dinner without complaining too much I would get a special Faratha cooked with a few spoonfuls of sugar rolled into the dough. This crisp and delicious bribe worked a treat!

According to my mum, Farathas are easy and no preservatives are necessary - which is rather reassuring isn't it?

Farathas go very nicely with Egg Chutney, Black Dal or are perfect with large helping of Cabbage and Potatoes.

Ingredients:

- 1/2 lb (250g) of plain flour
- A tablespoonful of cooking oil
- A small cup of warm water (5oz, 125ml)

This recipe will make 4-5 Farathas

DELICIOUS MAURITIUS

Method:

Add the flour to a large bowl.

Add the water. Mix everything together using your fingers until you are left with a soft dough. Knead the dough for a few minutes and it will become even softer. Pop the dough into a sealed Tupperware or similar and leave it to rest in the fridge for a minimum of an hour.

When you are ready to cook pinch off some dough. According to my mum it needs to be roughly the size of a satsuma, not a children's lunchbox sized one, a big one. Roll this out onto a floured board into a rough circle shape. Roll it out everywhere, making sure that you get right to the edges and that they are nice and thin. You are aiming to roll it out so that it is slightly smaller than a dinner plate. The thinner you can get the better. So roughly 2 mm thick everywhere. Make sure you use plenty of flour on your rolling pin and board so that it doesn't get stuck.

Put your hot plate or frying pan to heat on a medium heat. Too hot and your faratha will get burnt. Slap the Faratha flat onto the frying pan using a fish slice to help you. You need to leave it cook for about 1 - 1 1/2 minutes like this. You will begin to see some white bubbles rising to the surface. After this time, turn it over using the fish slice. Now, using your bush, lightly brush the Faratha with oil and turn it over again and repeat. It will turn a lovely light brown colour. You will know it is cooked when it turns light brown. Take this Faratha, fold it in half, and then in half again until you have a squarish shape, slam it with the palm of your hand (I am not entirely sure why this is done, but it is) and serve immediately.

Puri

Pronounced Pou-rie

Puris are round, puffy and very tasty. They are also soft, oily, served in stacks and are a must at weddings and at other important Mauritian ceremonies. You will want to cook at least 4 or 5 per person for dinner. Like their older first cousin the Faratha, you use them to eat sauces, curries and other delightful things. I love to eat them with Pumpkin, Cabbage and Kutchoo.

Ingredients:

- My mum tells me to put 1/2 pound of plain white or wholemeal flour. Either tastes nice. You could always try mixing a bit of both.
- 4.5 oz Warm water
- 1 Tablespoonful of vegetable oil, like corn oil. Not olive oil as it won't taste good.
- Plenty of vegetable oil to fry 1/2 pint will be a good start

This will make 9 - 10 purees

Method:

Sieve the flour if you want, and put it into a mixing bowl.

Add the oil to the flour and mix this into the flour using your hands until you make breadcrumbs.

Add the water to the breadcrumbs and mix this until you have a medium dough. This dough must not be very soft (as you would

DELICIOUS MAURITIUS

make with Faratha) but harder, so that it wont be too sticky, but soft enough to roll. Knead this dough well and leave it for half an hour in the fridge (if the weather is hot it will start to soften the dough and it will be very difficult to work with.

After 1/2 an hour take the dough out of the fridge. Have 1 table spoonful of oil standing by in a saucer.

Pinch off a ping pong ball size of the dough and make a round ball of it between your palms.

Pop this ball of dough onto a dry plate and repeat this whole process until you have used up all of the dough - you might need more than one plate for this.

Dip the ball of dough gently into the saucer of oil so that the bottom bit of the dough has a bit of oil on it. Now you need to roll the dough into a circle roughly the size of a saucer. The bit of oil will prevent it from sticking the rolling pin or the board. It will be quite thin but don't worry. Take the rolled out dough and put this onto a plate.

Repeat this process until you have rolled out about 3 or 4 Puris. Try not to have too many stacked up on top of each other or they will stick to each other. Use lots of different plates until you have rolled out everything.

Now in a wok or frying pan, put about 1/2 a pint of oil to warm, it will take about 5 minutes on a medium flame to heat up. You know when it has reached the correct temperature when the oil starts to smoke a little.

Pick up one of the Puris. Ease it gently into the hot oil, imagine you're immersing yourself slowly into a lovely warm bath - you don't want to make a big splash. Let it bubble and fry for about 1 minute. Using a slotted spoon carefully turn the Puri over. Cook it on this side for another minute. It will turn a light brown colour - careful to not let it go too dark. If all is well the Puri will be all puffed up and round, like a little football or a toddler's face! Take it out of the oil carefully using a slotted spoon, making sure that you don't take out too much oil.

Put the cooked Puri onto a plate which is lined with kitchen towel to absorb the excess oil and get started on making the next one. As the vapour leaves the cooked Puri, the puffiness will flatten - don't worry it will still taste very nice.

Puris can be eaten hot or cold.

Bootiful Bread Rolls

Pronounced just as you would imagine

According to my mum if you follow this recipe, you will be rewarded with deliciously puffed bread rolls that are lighter than a baby's bootee.

This recipe will make 4 rolls.

Ingredients:

- 1 cup - 1/2 lb of bread flour
- 1 tablespoonful of yeast powder
- 1 teaspoonful of sugar
- 1 teaspoonful of salt
- 1 tablespoonful of vegetable oil
- 15 tablespoonfuls of warm water

Method:

Add your flour to a mixing bowl. Add the salt, sugar, yeast, oil and water. Mix everything together with your hands and start to knead it to make a dough.

Don't worry about how soft the dough is, just keep kneading it for 8 minutes.

After the kneading you will be left with a lovely soft, elastic dough.

Cover your mixing bowl with a lid and leave it in a warm place for 1 hour.

The dough will have expanded, so you need to knock it back. Dust your hands with a little flour and knead it again for a minute or so.

Divide the dough into 4 and shape them into balls.

Put each ball onto a greased baking tray and let them rise again for another 1/2 hour. Preheat the oven to 250.

Put your rolls to bake in the preheated oven for 15 minutes.

I think that these are best eaten straight from the oven, hot and smeared with butter.

Party Snacks and Assorted Nibbles

Mauritian people love any excuse to celebrate with festive snacks. A birthday celebration simply isn't done without a few Samosas, munched steaming hot, wrapped in kitchen roll to keep your fingers from scorching. A plateful of soft Bhajias - served with a saucer of tomato ketchup is a perfect way to welcome your guests from overseas.

- Gram
- Vegetable Samosas
- Fish Samosas
- Lamb Samosas
- Kaka Pison (yes I am afraid that you did read that right!)
- Gateau Piment
- Kurhi
- Gateau Brinzel
- Bhajia
- Prawn Bhajia

A Moonlit Mauritian Party

One Christmas Eve we were invited to a party at a beach hut on Trou Aux Biches - a lovely name for a beach don't you think? Trou Aux Biches is roughly translated as Doe Hole, I imagine because the sand there is so soft and the water extremely mild. A small crowd of friends and relatives gathered together that evening and my cousin's wife Baby fried up batches of food from a wok set up right there on the beach.

The smoking oil of the bubbling wok reflected the lights strung up overhead. Plastic cups brimmed with Mauritian Rum and full fat Coke and the night air filled with tasty smells music and gossip. At one point we waded into the sea and sat my nephew Ravi - who was then still a baby - in a fishing boat that was illuminated by a single moon beam.

Later that evening we went for a stroll along the beach. As it was Christmas Eve a number of the hotel restaurants had set up some gorgeous tables pied a l'eau - that is to say the tables had been set out so that diners could feel the lap of the ocean about their feet whilst they ate their dinner. Fine crystal, glinting cutlery, and starched linens were all perfectly beautiful.

Ravi didn't want the party to end.

Tiny Shop

The tiny wooden shop was more of a shack really. A glass counter with warm chocolates amongst other treats. Sitting at the counter, legs swinging and sipping Fanta from a straw. Slipping off the soft pink skins of the lightly toasted peanuts.

Gram

Pronounced just as you would imagine

Gram is such a tasty snack! My mum told me that in Mauritius old people would stand outside schools at lunchtime and sell bags of this to hungry school children. A few spoonfuls of this is much healthier than a bag of crisps or a horrid box of chicken, don't you agree? The glistening onions add a little oily glamour to a very simple dish.

Ingredients:

- 1 cup (1/2 lb) of black or brown Gram (you can buy this in Indian shops) soaked in 2 pints of water overnight
- 1/2 onion
- 1 clove garlic, peeled and chopped
- 1 teaspoonful of salt
- 1 dried chilli, chopped into pieces
- 1/2 cup water
- 2 tablespoonfuls of vegetable oil

Method:

Discard the soaking water from the Gram. Their overnight soaking will transform them from dark brown shrivelled things to plumped up lovelies that are a pale golden-brown colour.

Add the Gram to your trusty pressure cooker. Add the water and salt, cover and let it boil on high and under pressure for 5 minutes. Check to see if it has softened by giving it a pinch. If if hasn't softened enough (it needs to be easy to crush between your fingers and have a slightly floury texture) add a couple more spoonfuls of water and allow them to boil under pressure (ding ding ding de de de dum) for another 5 minutes.

If when you uncover the pan you discover that the gram is swimming in a lot of excess water simply boil the whole lot uncovered until the water has evaporated.

Now, add the oil, onion garlic and chilli to the cooked gram and stir everything together over a low flame. Cover again and allow to cook with no pressure this time for 5 minutes, stirring occasionally.

The gram will be glistening and coated with the oil and onion mix. Perfect to munch on whilst watching a 4-hour long Bollywood movie.

Vegetable Samosas

If you want to pronounce it like my mum say Sam-O-Sa as quick as you can

Here is the best ever recipe for Samosas - honed by my mum over several decades. She's made them for pretty much every family birthday party and every other celebration in between. Crispy pastry triangles, filled with a moist mush of spiced and garlicky flavours, these are utterly utterly delicious.

This recipe will make 15 Samosas. Normal people with healthy appetites will eat up to two of these before dinner. If your family is anything like mine you will need many more.

Ingredients:

For the pad - this is the pastry wrapping for the Samosa.

- 1/2 lb of white plain flour. Don't make it with brown flour or no one will eat them.
- 1/2 cup of cold water
- Sprinkle of salt

How to make the Samosa pads:

Add the flour and water to a bowl and sprinkle in the salt. Mix this a spoon first and then finish up with your hands. According to my mum you are looking for a malleable soft dough consistency that is not runny, but still soft enough to roll out nicely. Sprinkle some flour onto a board.

Pinch off a ping pong ball sized bit of dough and roll this into a ball between your palms. If the dough sticks to your hands add a tiny bit of flour.

Now using a rolling pin, roll the ball into a rectangle about 5 x 7 inches in size. The dough needs to be thin, not quite as thin as filo pastry, maybe 1-2mm in depth. It is important that you stick quite closely to these measurements as you will be cutting the dough into strips later and if you don't roll it out wide enough you wont be able to cut the dough into big enough strips.

Put a hot plate or frying pan to warm on a medium flame. When its hot, pop the rolled out rectangle of dough onto it. Spin it round once, turn it over and spin it round once more. This should take 30 seconds in total. What you are trying to do here is to dry out the dough ever so slightly so that it is no longer sticky, but it is still pliable. This means that you will be able to stuff it with your filling with the greatest of ease. You are aiming for your pad to reach the consistency of a wrap, you are not trying to cook it at the moment - remember that it will be fried later on.

Set the toasted pad aside on a plate.

Repeat this process until you have finished off all of your dough, stacking up the pads one on top of another as you go.

Now, cut the pad lengthways along the middle so that you have 2 pieces per pad. These will be roughly 2.5 x 7 inches in measurement. Repeat this until you have cut all of the pads in this way.

Put the pads into a Tupperware box or in a plastic bag. This will prevent them from drying out too much.

Now we move on to making your delicious filling

Ingredients:

- 2 large potatoes or 5 small ones. Peeled and diced

- 1/2 cup of frozen peas. Please don't be tempted to use fresh peas. There is a time and place for fresh peas and this is not that time.
- 1/2 bunch of spring onion finely chopped
- 1/2 onion finely chopped
- 1/2 teaspoonful of salt
- A few sprigs of coriander, chopped
- 1 tablespoonful of curry powder
- 1/2 teaspoonful of turmeric powder

Method:

Boil the potatoes until they are almost cooked - use a fork to check. When you think that there are five more minutes before the potatoes are done add your frozen peas (if you really had to use fresh ones make sure that they are super tender). Bring the mixture back to the boil and cook for a further 5 minutes.

Once the potatoes are fully cooked and nice and fluffy, drain the water away from the potatoes and peas.

Now sprinkle the potatoes and peas with the salt, the spring onion, onion, coriander, curry and turmeric powder and mix together well. Make sure that the potatoes are well coated with everything else. The consistency needs to be soft and well mixed. Try to keep the peas as whole as possible and ensure that the mashed potato coats everything.

Now we need to make some paste that will glue your Samosa together

Paste ingredients:

- 1 teaspoonful of plain flour
- 1 1/2 teaspoonful of water

Method to make the paste:

Mix the two things together until you have a runny paste. As this is going to stick the Samosa together it needs to be slightly gloopy in texture - not too thick and not too runny.

Now comes the fun bit. You are going to assemble your Samosa. Take a deep breath, it is a lot easier than you think…

You are aiming to make a triangular cone pocket out of it that has a flap at the top. Imagine that you are making a party hat out of a piece of paper and you're aiming in the right sort of direction.

Now, take a tablespoonful of your potato mixture and put this into the pocket, making sure that you hold it tight so the filling doesn't spill everywhere.

Dip your finger into the flour glue paste and rub this over the inside edge of the flap bit.

Now close the pocket into a neat triangle and congratulations you have successfully constructed a Samosa! Set this aside in a large mixing bowl.

Repeat this process until all of the pads have been filled up in this way and you have used up all of your filling mixture. You will have a large bowl filled with neat triangular pastries all ready to be cooked.

How to fry your Samosas:

Heat up a cup of vegetable oil in a sturdy wok - a large frying pan will also do the trick. When this oil has heated up nicely you add your Samosa to cook. Nicely heated up oil means that it has started to smoke ever so slightly. Carefully add as many Samosas to the pan as possible so that they all are able to cook evenly on one side at a time. You might like to lower them in using a slotted spoon. My mum generally uses her fingers because hers are heatproof. In a regular frying pan of roughly 30 cm, you can cook 6 Samosas at one time. It will take around 5 minutes to cook on one side. Using a slotted spoon, turn them all over starting with the first Samosa that went in to the oil and continue until all of them have been turned. Fry for another 5 minutes until they are golden and bubbly - definitely not brown. If they go brown they won't taste good at all. Golden, ok?

Remove the golden brown Samosas from the oil using your trusty slotted spoon and put them onto a plate lined with a few sheets of kitchen towel to absorb the excess oil.

Repeat this until you have cooked all of the Samosas in this way.

Samosas are best eaten boiling hot, wrapped in some kitchen towel under the pretence of "Tasting for Salt". You will definitely burn your mouth.

Variations on Samosas

In addition to the very delicious vegetable Samosa, there are a few variations of fillings that you can try. How about Lamb or fish Samosas? Both are good, although it is worth thinking about what you will be serving for your main course. You don't want to overload with meat or fish.

Fish Samosas

According to my mum these will taste fishy and tasty (I should hope so too!). Red snapper is such a flavoursome fish and its texture is just about perfect.

Ingredients:

- 2 red snappers, cleaned with no head (according to my mum you can make a soup with the head. I'm just letting you know that I won't be going anywhere near that soup)
- 1 onion, chopped finely
- 2 springs of spring onion
- 1 tablespoonful of curry powder
- 1 little teaspoonful of turmeric
- 1 potato, peeled, diced and boiled
- 1/2 small cup of frozen peas, boiled
- Salt to taste
- A cup or so of vegetable oil for frying

Method:

Heat the oil in a frying pan and fry the red snappers for 7 minutes on each side until the skin has gone crispy and the fish is cooked through completely. Remove from the pan and set aside to cool uncovered on a plate.

Once the fish is cool enough to handle get to work carefully removing the skin and the bones. Discard these and mash up the fish using a fork until it forms small flakes.

Add the rest of the ingredients: and mix together well until everything is combined and coated. Drizzle over a spoonful of vegetable oil and stir through.

Fill your Samosas as above and cook in exactly the same way as the vegetable ones.

Lamb Samosas

If a Cornish pasty went on holiday to Mauritius, this rich and filling Lamb Samosa would be the result!

- 1 lb minced lamb (this is a small packet)
- 1 onion, chopped finely
- 2 springs of spring onion
- 1 tablespoonful of curry powder
- 1 little teaspoonful of turmeric
- 1 clove of garlic (if you want)
- 1 potato, peeled, diced and boiled
- 1/2 small cup of frozen peas, boiled
- Salt to taste

Method:

Add a tiny drizzle of oil to a heavy frying pan and heat this over a medium flame until hot.

Once the pan is hot add the minced lamb and cook for about 10 minutes stirring occasionally.

After 10 minutes the minced lamb will look dark brown and will smell gorgeous. The lamb mince however will be surrounded by liquid fat which you will need to discard or the Samosas will be far too heavy. Here is how you do it: Sit a colander over a plate and spoon the piping hot lamb into the colander. Using a spoon or spatula press the lamb down into the colander. This will squeeze the excess fat out onto the plate. Once this cools down it will solidify and you can easily discard it in your bin. Don't be tempted to pour this liquid fat down your sink otherwise you will have a blocked sink, a blocked drain and everything will start to stink and you won't be able to do your washing up ever again.

Put the onions into the frying pan, add the defatted lamb, and mix this together with the rest of the ingredients. Let this cook gently for a couple of minutes until the onion has softened slightly.

Your lamb filling is finished. Assemble and cook as normal.

Sega Dancing

Sega music originated amongst the slave populations of Mauritius. It is the island's official dance, unique because when you dance it properly your feet don't leave the floor - you drag them along in a shuffle instead. I discovered recently that this special movement recollects the difficulty of dancing whilst wearing the heavy shackles of slavery. The focus of the Sega dance is in the hips which pulse in time to the beat of a drum. Very young and very old Mauritians all know how to dance this instinctively - it flows through our blood.

Quite close to the gleaming shopping centres of Port Louis harbour is Aapravasi Ghat. A couple of small shacks and uneven stone floors make it an unlikely UNESCO World Heritage centre. Aapravasi Ghat is important because it marks the site where people disembarked from ships to work as paid indentured labourers on the plantations of Mauritius. This means that they would receive money in exchange for their labour instead of working as slaves. There is a quiet and melancholy energy about the place - my mum told me once that she goes to that place when she wants to feel sad.

A Tale of Two Birdies

The dodo was a simple flightless bird that was endemic to the island of Mauritius. With no natural predators dodo didn't need to fly and instead chilled out, drank beer and slowly turned to pot. These big birds (astonishingly they grew up to 3ft tall!) had giant heads topped off with a handsome curled beak. Sadly for them they must have tasted delicious because by the end of the 17th Century the poor dodo had been hunted to extinction by hoards of hungry sailors.

It looked like history was going to repeat itself in the 1970s when the Pink Pigeon, another bird endemic to Mauritius looked like it was going the same way as its flightless cousin. Due to extensive habitat loss and the impact of introduced mammalian predators there were only a dozen of these birds left. Happily following an intensive recovery program the pink pigeon crisis - which one might call a Kaka-Pison - has been averted.

Kaka Pison

Pronounced Ka-Ka Piz-on

Kaka Pison is literally translated as pigeon poo - which is a terribly unappetising name for something so crunchily tasty! Think of Kaka Pison as home made Bombay mix - perfect to peck on during never ending episodes of the Mahabharat. In addition to imparting a special aroma and subtle taste, the ajwan seeds contain enzymes that help to improve digestion.

Ingredients:

- 1/2 lb of besan gram flour
- 1 teaspoonful of salt
- 1/4 teaspoonful of baking soda
- 1 tablespoonful of vegetable oil
- 1/4 cup water
- 1/4 teaspoonful of ajwan seeds
- 1/4 teaspoonful of chilli powder
- 2 cups of vegetable oil for frying
- 1 sprig of curry leaves

You will need to have a special grinder, a little bit like a potato ricer, with very small holes. You can buy these from Indian shops.

Method:

Mix all of the ingredients - apart from the curry leaves - together until you have created a firm, pale yellow dough. This will not take long.

Put the oil to heat up in a wok over a medium flame.

Take the dough and add it to your special grinder - a potato ricer would do the trick if you don't have one of these yourself. The holes can be anything between 1 - 5mm - it is up to you.

When the oil is hot enough, squeeze the dough out into the hot oil by turning the handle of your special machine, or squeezing it out of your potato ricer into the hot oil. Do this so that the surface of the wok is covered with your mixture, don't go over more than once.

The dough will sink slightly and then rise up to the surface when it is cooked and darken slightly. After a minute, turn it over, cook again for another minute, remove from the oil and drain on kitchen paper.

When you have cooked all of your Kaka Pison, throw your curry leaves into the boiling oil. Let them fry for a minute, and then remove from the oil and set aside on a plate to cool. The leaves will have crisped up beautifully. When they are cool enough to handle, crumble them over your Kaka Pison. The aroma will be wonderful!

Your snack is ready to eat straight away. If you want to, you can throw in some toasted cashews and peanuts.

The Mystery Of The Floating Gateau Piment

A fitting end to a blazing hot summer's day is a trip to Perebere Beach. And so my cousin Ramesh and I decided that this is exactly where we should go. We anticipated an afternoon of healthy sport, swimming and splashing in the sheltered Perebere lagoon.

Backstroking languidly across the lagoon that was when I saw it. Someone had obviously been careless at lunch. The pale-brown deep-fried treat bobbed along innocently in the crystal clear water. And then it happened to bob by a little bit closer…When it was revealed to not be a floating gateau piment at all, but a floater of a very different and most unsavoury kind.

"Everyone out" bellowed Ramesh.

Gateau Piment

Pronounced Gat - Oh Peem-eh
Chilli Cakes

If the earnest falafel had a glamorous makeover it might transform into a Gateaux Piment. These crisp, sun kissed and chilli-hot bites are adored by Mauritian people of all ages - if you plan to serve them to children you might like to cut out the chilli and they will still be delicious. In my opinion Gateaux Piment are best served Hot Hot Hot which incidentally is a song by a band called Arrow that has been played at every single Mauritian wedding all over the world since the 1980s. They are a wonderful breakfast dish and also make smashing pre-dinner snacks. My mum makes them as flattish rings with a hole in the middle, but you can fashion them into simple ball shapes and they will taste equally gorgeous.

This recipe will make 20 Gateaux Piments

Ingredients:

- 1 small cupful of chickpeas (you can make it with channa dal, but my mum things that it is tastier made with chickpeas), soaked overnight in a pan of cold water.
- 1/2 onion, very finely chopped
- 1 or 2 chillis (When my mum made these for her next door neighbours she left this out so that their little girl could eat them, so feel free to add as much or as little as you like)
- 3 individual spring onions (not 3 bunches, 3 individual onions) finely chopped

- 4 or 5 individual strands of fresh coriander, including the leaves, finely chopped
- 1 teaspoonful of salt
- Pinch of bicarbonate - this will help everything to puff up as they cook
- 1 cup of vegetable oil to fry

Method:

Firstly drain the chickpeas into a colander. Now grind these using a blender or a pestle and mortar. You don't want everything to be too uniform in texture, you want there to be a few larger bits here and there to add texture.

Put your roughly ground chickpeas in a bowl and add in all of the ingredients: (minus obviously the cup of oil) and stir this up well. It will have a lovely fresh aroma and will be a yellowy cream colour.

Put your oil into a wok and let this heat up over a medium flame until the oil starts to smoke.

Once the oil starts to smoke you are ready to fry.

Pinch off a small amount of the chickpea mixture, roughly the size of 1/2 a ping pong ball. Now flatten this ball slightly between the palm of your hands so that it becomes a slightly flattened ball. Push your finger into the centre of this shape to create either a hole or a slight indent. This will help it to cook slightly quicker as well as looking pretty.

Once you have fashioned your shape (Like I said earlier, please don't worry if you cant make these punctured rings, simply roll the mixture into a ball and they will taste marvellous) drop it carefully into the hot oil using your fingers. Be careful - you don't want oil to splash onto your party frock. Pop around 7 or 8 of these beauties into the oil at one time and turn them occasionally until they become a gorgeous golden brown colour. They will take roughly 2 minutes to cook on each side, so your cooking time for one batch is around 4 minutes. Don't let them go too dark or instead of being sun kissed your Gateaux Piments will be sunburned and no one will want to go near them

Remove your golden Gateaux from the oil with a slotted spoon, drain off as much excess oil as you can back into the wok, and add them to a plate covered with several sheets of kitchen paper to absorb any remaining excess cooking oil.

Continue until you have finished frying your batch. If for some reason you don't want to eat the lot your uncooked mixture will keep perfectly happily in the fridge for a few days.

Gateaux Piments are delicious to eat on their own or with a dip and taste particularly good when eaten at a party. You can also pop a few of these into a well buttered bit of baguette and have a Gateaux Piments sandwich. The butter melts and every bite tastes of sunshine and the seaside and happy times.

A variation on Gateau Piment: Kurhi

Pronounced Kur-He

This moist and moreish dish is made with Gateaux Piments as the starting point. The crisp and crunchy Gateaux absorbs its lightly spiced sauce and becomes a softly luscious dish that is light yet very satisfying. This recipe will happily serve 2 people with very big appetites and it keeps very well for a few days in the fridge.

Ingredients:

Use the recipe above to make the Gateaux Piments. Now let's make the curry sauce for which you will need:

- 1/2 onion
- 4 strands of coriander, chopped finely
- 1 tablespoonful of curry powder
- 1 teaspoonful of turmeric
- 1 teaspoonful of salt
- 1/4 can of tinned tomatoes
- 2 cloves of garlic, crushed and finely chopped
- 1/2 inch cube of ginger, very finely grated
- 2 tablespoonfuls of yoghurt
- 2 tablespoonfuls of oil
- 4-5 curry leaves if you can get them

DELICIOUS MAURITIUS

Method:

Prepare the Gateau Piments as above with a few key tweaks:

Instead of the flattened space ship shapes with the hole in the middle fashion them into small ball shapes around 3 cm diameter. Also, you don't want to fry them too much - they just need to take on a try bit of colour. They will finish cooking later on in their bath of curry sauce. Fry them for 1- 1½ minutes on each side, so 3 minutes in total.

Once cooked remove from the hot oil and set aside on a plate covered in several sheets of kitchen paper.

On to the sauce:

In a saucepan, gently fry the chopped onion in the oil over a low flame. Fry for about 2 minutes until the onion has softened. Now add all of the spices, salt and and curry leaves, ginger and garlic and tomato. Mix this together well and cook gently for 2 -3 minutes until the tomato is nice and soft.

Add 1 teacupful of cold water, stir it well and bring it to the boil uncovered under a medium flame. Once the sauce has boiled properly for 5 minutes - it has to boil properly - then you add the cooked Gateau Piment and let everything cook together, making sure that all of the gateaux balls are covered with the sauce. Connect with your maternal side and treat them gently as you don't want them to break up. Let everything cook together uncovered in this way for 1 minute.

Now turn the heat off, add the yoghurt and gently stir this into the sauce. Add the chopped coriander and again stir this in with a graceful lightness of touch.

Finally, cover the pan and leave for 5 - 10 minutes. During this time the Gateau Piments will soak up all of the delicious sauce, so try to resist digging in and eating it immediately - it tastes better if you leave it for at least 10 minutes.

Serve this splendid dish simply with plain rice which will soak up the rest of the sauce. You don't need anything else to accompany it - as my marvellous brother in law Patrick is fond of saying: You don't want to over egg the pudding.

Gateaux Brinzels

Pronounced Gat-oh Braa-Zel

Gateaux Brinzels are delightfully moist slices of aubergine fried in batter. The aubergine goes squidgy, the batter goes crisp and together they create a rather splendid mid afternoon snack - perfect with a squeeze of ketchup or a spoonful of chutney. You will need to track down a special sort of aubergine to make this this: The ideal one will be round in shape and roughly the size of an orange.

Ingredients:

- 1 round aubergine. This needs to be cut into round slices about 1/2 cm thick
- 1/2 onion or 1 shallot finely diced
- 1 chilli finely chopped
- 1 clove of garlic, chopped finely
- 1/2 inch cube of ginger, grated
- A few sprigs of fresh coriander, finely chopped
- 2 tablespoonfuls of self raising flour
- 1 cupful of besan flour
- 1/2 cup of cold water
- 1/2 teaspoonful of salt
- 1 cup of vegetable oil for frying

Method:

Lightly sprinkle each aubergine slice with the salt - make sure that you don't overdo it. Place the slices onto a plate and set aside.

Pour the water into a bowl. Add to this the self raising flour, salt, and besan flour and mix everything together to make a paste. It mustn't be too runny as you want this paste to cling to the aubergine slices. If it looks like it is a bit too runny, add a little more Besan flour. If it's too thick, add a bit more water a little at a time. You are aiming to produce something with the texture of a thick pancake batter.

Now throw in your coriander, chilli, onion, garlic and ginger and stir thoroughly. Leave this to stand for 1/2 hour.

Put a frying pan to heat over a medium flame and add the vegetable oil. Heat this until it gives off a little smoke.

Take some kitchen towel and pat dry the individual aubergine slices. You'll remove a slightly brownish liquid that the salt has helped to extract.

Dip the aubergine into the batter mixture and make sure that it is coated evenly. Now gently place it into the hot oil. Slowly slowly does it. Repeat until you have about 4 pieces of the aubergine in the pan. It's important to not overfill the pan as it will become tricky to turn them over if it's too crowded.

Fry for about 1½ - 2 minutes per side until they have reached a glorious golden colour. Use a metal slotted spoon to turn them over and be careful not to splash. Once cooked remove from the oil and transfer onto a plate lined with kitchen paper to draw off the excess oil. Repeat until you have fried everything.

Eat these beauties with a dollop of coriander or coconut chutney. J'adore avec ketchup!

Bhajia

Pronounced Bha-Jee-a

These are soft, golden clouds of deliciousness far, far removed from the parched and scorched supermarket Onion Bhajis that you might have eaten from time to time. When the Bhajia batter hits the hot oil it puffs up creating a light and fluffy snack speckled with flecks of moist onion. My mum whips up batches of these in minutes, and offers them to us with some home made mint chutney or a saucer of shop bought tomato ketchup on the side.

Ingredients:

- 1 onion finely diced
- 2 spring onions (*not* 2 bunches) chopped finely
- 2 chillis finely chopped
- 2 cloves of garlic, chopped finely
- 1/2 inch cube of ginger, grated
- 3 -4 sprigs of fresh coriander, finely chopped
- 2 tablespoonfuls of self raising flour
- 2 cupfuls of besan flour (300g)
- 3/4 cup of cold water (300ml)
- 1 teaspoonful of salt
- 2 cups of vegetable oil for frying

Method:

Mix all of the ingredients (apart from the oil, obviously) together to make a soft batter. You are aiming to create a batter the texture of sponge cake batter. A spoonful of this should drop off the spoon softly and slowlily.

Heat up your vegetable oil in a wok under a medium flame. Once the oil starts to smoke gently you are ready to wok and roll.

Take a tablespoonful of the batter and gently drop this into the hot oil. Repeat this 10 times until you have a wok full of cooking bhajias floating in the hot oil. Don't put in too many if you are new to this as you might start to worry about how on earth you will get them out in time.

Turn the bhajias over from time to time until all sides have turned a golden ochre colour. They will also puff up and become very round. Make sure that you don't let them go too dark or they will not taste right. When they are done remove from the oil using a metal slotted spoon and allow to drain on several sheets of kitchen towel.

Prawn Bhajia

If you have some shelled and deveined prawns to hand, either cooked or raw, you can dip these into the batter and spoon them out into the hot oil. Cook them for the same amount of time. It is a lovely surprise to bite into an occasional steamy prawn!

Dips and Chutneys

Mauritian people love chutneys. Sometimes these will be made by simply blending together a handful of herbs, at other times they will require slightly more assembly - but not much. When sprinkled with a spoonful of chutney even the most humble of foods starts to smell and taste sublime.

- Coconut Chutney
- Simple Coriander Chutney
- Shrimp Chutney
- Salt Fish Chutney
- Mint Chutney
- Roast Aubergine Chutney
- Simple Tomato Chutney
- Egg Chutney
- Home Made Plain Yoghurt
- Raita

Coconut Chutney

Coconut chutney is a slightly smoky and tangy condiment that adds instant richness to your meal. My mum used to get me to crack the coconut by hurling it on the floor. If you are less dramatic than my mum you could always crack open your coconut by carefully tapping the shell all around its circumference with a heavy knife.

Ingredients:

- You will need a coconut
- 10 sprigs of coriander (this is a small bunch)
- 5 green or red chillis, yes you read that correctly.
- 1 heaped tablespoonful of tamarind, either fresh or boxed, with any stones removed.
- 4 - 5 cloves of garlic (again, your eyes were not deceiving you)
- 1/2 teaspoonful of salt

Method:

Remove half of the flesh from the coconut and roughly grate it. It doesn't have to be super finely grated as you will be blending it later on. Now add the grated coconut to a dry frying pan and allow it to toast over a medium flame until it turns a light brown colour and the aroma becomes warm and rich. Remove from the heat.

When the toasted coconut is cool put this into a blender and grind it until it has the consistency of dry semolina. Now add the coriander, chilli, tamarind, garlic and salt to the and whizz everything around for about 1 minute. It will be a light green brown colour. The longer you bend it the smoother it will be.

Add to a bowl and serve with a spoon

Simple Coriander Chutney

This is easy to make. It smells very fresh and clean and is a beautiful bright green colour. It is very tasty. My mum cautions you against adding too much tomato or everything will taste watery. This recipe will make a bowl full.

Ingredients:

- 1/2 bunch of coriander
- 4 - 5 very hot chillis
- 2 - 3 tomatoes depending on the size. If you are using tiny tomatoes then put about 6.
- 5 cloves of garlic
- 1/2 teaspoonful of tamarind if you like
- Salt to taste

Method:

I repeat, this is very easy. Cut everything up roughly, squash the garlic a bit, crush the coriander up a bit. Put everything into your blender and then blend until you have a rough paste. That is it. Pour into your bowl and get dipping!

Shrimp Chutney

Although this chutney is simple to prepare it is an extremely elegant condiment which you might consider serving from a particularly pretty bowl.

Ingredients:

- 1/8 pound of fresh river shrimps. They are very tiny, they are up to 1 inch in length. They sell them everywhere in Mauritius but you'll have to hunt for them in the UK. You will be eating them all up, including their shells, so make sure that you give them a good clean.
- 3 chillis
- Salt to taste
- 2-3 cloves of garlic
- An onion, roughly chopped
- 2 tablespoonfuls of vegetable oil
- 3 tomatoes

Method:

Wash the shrimps nicely in a pan and drain out the water. Pat them dry with a tea towel that you don't mind smelling of fish.

Heat a dry frying pan. Add the shrimps to this and toast them. They will turn pink which signals that they are now cooked. Take them out and let them cool down a bit.

Add the cooked and cooled river shrimp to a blender and blend them until they are a rough paste. Set this aside in a bowl.

Now aside from the onion, blend the rest of the ingredients together.

Take a large frying pan heat up your vegetable oil. Fry the left out chopped onion in here, stirring it from time to time until it goes light brown and transparent. Add the blended shrimp paste to this and let it fry together with the onion for 2 -3 minutes. The mixture will darken to a medium brown colour as it cooks.

Add the rest of the blended ingredients to the frying pan and cook together on a medium heat for 4 minutes. You will need to stir this regularly to prevent sticking.

Taste the shrimp chutney. If it needs a little more oil sprinkle on a little more.

Et Voila! It's done. You can eat this either hot or cold and it will keep happily in the fridge for up to a week.

Salt Fish Chutney

According to my mum only those who have been exposed to the pungent flavour of this chutney since childhood will be able to tolerate the taste of this. She is incorrect about this. I was exposed to it as a child and still run from it as far and as fast as my little legs will carry me. People with more sophisticated palates than mine however absolutely love it.

A note: Salt fish does have a very lingering, pungent aroma so when you cook it ensure that all window are wide open.

A hope: That you have an extractor fan.

This serves 4 people.

Ingredients:

- 1 large onion, finely chopped
- 1 chilli, chopped
- 3 tomatoes, chopped
- 3 cloves of garlic, crushed and chopped
- A spit of thyme
- 1/2 teaspoonful of salt
- 4 tablespoonfuls of oil
- 1/2 lb of salt fish - my mum recommends snook fish or cod

Method:

Open the windows.

First you need to rehydrate your salt fish. Soak the fish in boiling water and leave covered for for 10 minutes. Discard the water and repeat this process 3 times.

Put 2 tablespoonfuls of oil to a frying pan, heat over a medium flame and then add the rehydrated fish. Fry this gently, turning occasionally for 5 minutes. The fish will brown but will not go too crispy. Set the fish aside.

Add the rest of the oil to the frying pan and warm over a medium flame. Add the onion and allow this to fry for 2 minutes until it softens. Now add the garlic chilli tomato thyme and salt. Lower the flame, cover and allow to simmer for 5 minutes until the tomato has softened.

Check that you have removed any remaining bones from the fish and add this to the tomato sauce. Add 2 spoonfuls of water to the sauce, cover and cook again on a low heat for 2-3 minutes.

Close the windows and good luck!

Mint Chutney

Fresh tasting and fragrant Mint Chutney couldn't be simpler to make. If you cover and refrigerate any leftovers it will keep perfectly well for a couple of days.

Ingredients:

- 1 bunch of mint
- 1/2 bunch of dhania (that is the Mauritian word for coriander)
- 4 normal sized tomatoes
- 1 level teaspoonful of salt
- 1 tablespoonful of tamarind (make sure that you don't have stones in it)
- 4 hot chillis (5 if you like it very hot. Or 6 if you really want to get things moving)
- 4 cloves of garlic
- 1 tablespoonful of lemon juice if you like

Method:

Chop the tomatoes roughly.

If the mint has particularly hard stems you can remove them.

Wash and roughly chop the dhania.

Peel your garlic

Put all of the ingredients into the blender and whizz until it reaches a roughly ground consistency. About 30 seconds should do it.

Fin

Roast Aubergine Chutney

You can eat this chutney as an accompaniment to a main course. It's also a perfect barbecue dip and nice with nachos too. When god was handing out good looks to chutneys, Roast Aubergine Chutney was sadly at the bottom of the queue - It is a rather unappetising grey colour and has a slightly bogey-ish appearance. Happily its taste and aroma more than make up for its appearance - it is smoky, sour and rather yummy.

This recipe will make enough for a small bowlful, enough to split with 4 - 6 people.

Ingredients:

- 1 large aubergine
- 2 medium onions finely chopped
- 2 chillis finely chopped (or 1, if you don't like it too hot)
- 3 cloves of garlic crushed and grated finely
- 2 tablespoonfuls of olive oil
- 1 teaspoonful of salt
- 4 sprigs of coriander, chopped finely
- Juice of 1/2 lemon

Method:

Prick your aubergine all over with a fork, slice it down the middle, and put it in a hot preheated oven, cut side down. Allow this to roast for a few minutes until its skin has blackened and charred. Remove from the oven and allow to cool slightly.

When the aubergine is cool enough to handle, peel off the charred skin. The aubergine will have changed consistency and gone all gooey and soft. Put this into a bowl and using a fork mash this up well.

Add the onion, garlic, salt, olive oil, lemon juice and chilli and stir them all together.

It's done! If you want to serve this cool, leave in the fridge for an hour or so, or it is perfect as it is.

A variation on this recipe is to leave out the lemon juice and to add 2 tablespoonfuls of plain yoghurt.

Simple Tomato Chutney

Unlike the other chutneys I've mentioned this one is served hot. It is very good to eat and it is particularly nice with a nice warm faratha. This cheery, bright red chutney is vegan which makes it perfect for a fasting day or when you feel like giving your system a bit of a rest.

This will make enough for 2 people

Ingredients:

- 4 ripe tomatoes
- 1 onion
- 1 or 2 cloves of garlic
- 1 hot chilli
- A sprig or 2 of fresh thyme. When she made this for us my mum would get me to pluck this from the garden. If you don't have thyme a sprinkling of mixed herbs will do nicely.
- Salt to taste
- 2 tablespoonfuls of vegetable oil

Method:

Cut up your onions so that they are sliced or diced around 1 cm wide

Cut up the tomatoes roughly

Slice the chilli along the middle

Grate the garlic

Wash the thyme

In a frying pan, heat the oil. When the oil is hot gently fry the onions until they are a light brown colour. You are aiming for a soft consistency, not crisp.

Now, add everything else to the pan, reduce the flame to low then cook until all of the tomatoes have gone soft. This will take around 10 minutes.

Eat on its own or you can use this chutney as the basis for a lamb or chicken daube.

Egg Chutney

This recipe will serve 2 people. Try it with some plain boiled rice, a faratha or a couple of warm puris. Colourful and tangy this simple and speedy meal takes no time whip up after work.

Ingredients:

- 3 eggs
- Tomato chutney - as above

Method:

Crack and whip up the eggs. Fry in a small pan and turn over. Cook for a couple of minutes until perfectly golden and it is no longer runny.

Put the cooked omelette into the tomato chutney. Leave it to cook together for a couple of minutes. The egg will absorb some of the tomato juice.

Serve immediately.

Home Made Plain Yoghurt

Yoghurt isn't strictly a chutney but you do dollop it on the side of your plate so that's why its included here. Use as a condiment to cool down a hot curry. This yoghurt has a fromage frais texture and is very simple to make.

Ingredients:

- 2 teaspoonful of plain live yoghurt
- 1 pint of full fat milk

Method:

Heat the milk very slowly over a low flame and bring it to boil. There is no need to stir or touch it in any way, and heating it over a low flame means that it will not boil over, so if you are not a very confident cook this recipe is right for you.

When it has boiled, pour the boiling milk into a small stainless steel bowl. It needs to have a lid.

Alternatively, if your milk pan is stainless steel you can simply pop its lid on top.

Now dollop the yoghurt in to the hot milk. Don't stir it around, just dollop it in. Like I said before, this recipe is perfect for a beginner. Cover up your pan, wrap it up in a warm towel and put it to rest in a warm place. An airing cupboard is perfect.

When you return 8 hours later it will be done - prepare this Yoghurt at night time and it will be ready for your breakfast in the morning. It will have changed consistency and have set.

Eat immediately or stored in the fridge for a few days.

Raita

Raita is a cooling yoghurt based relish, a soothing foil for a spicy curry or tandoori dish. A splash of this makes even the most humble of meals feel like a special occasion. If you really want to make a splash, throw in some pomegranate seeds.

Ingredients:

- 1 small tub of plain yoghurt (or make your own!)
- 1 cucumber prepared in a particular way (read on for instructions)
- Couple of sprigs of mint, chopped
- Sprinkle of salt to taste
- 1 pomegranate, with all of the seeds and pith removed - optional

Method:

First prepare your cucumber - this is done in a special way. First you need to peel it, then cut it horizontally into 2 inch chunks. Taking a small knife, carefully cut into the cucumber and cut around it into 1/2 cm or smaller spirals until you reach the seeds in the middle. Eat these. It's thirsty work. You will be left with a ringlet of cucumber. Now roll this up into a tight curl and slice this ringlet horizontally into 1/2 cm slices. Repeat until you have done this to all of the cucumber. I once tried to cut corners by grating it. It looked like a big mass of soggy bogey. Please learn from my mistake.

Add the cucumber, sprinkle with the chopped mint and salt and there it is. If you are feeling particularly Rubylicious, add the pomegranate.

Serve this immediately as if will go watery and start to separate if you leave it too long.

Meat

When I was growing up the only beef that we would eat is the occasional beef burger. We didn't eat pork at all. So that is why the meat recipes here are mainly for chicken and lamb which we ate every day apart from Monday. Venison was saved for very special occasions indeed!

- Tandoori Chicken
- Lamb Curry
- Lamb Daube
- Chicken Curry
- Venison Curry

Tandoori Chicken

This is my mum's Mauritian take on traditional Indian tandoori chicken. This recipe will make enough for 4 people.

Ingredients:

- 4 skinned chicken legs together with their thighs (these are the most moist bits)
- 3 cloves of garlic, crushed and chopped
- 1 inch cube of ginger, grated finely
- 1 teaspoonful of chilli powder
- 2 tablespoonfuls of tandoori masala
- 1 teaspoonful of salt
- 2 tablespoonfuls of plain yoghurt
- 1 tablespoonful of vegetable oil
- A bunch of coriander, finely chopped
- 1/2 lemon, squeezed

Method:

If you are squeamish, buy your chicken legs ready skinned. Skinning chicken is not a job for anyone without a) a strong stomach and b) a strong grip. If in doubt, buy your chicken ready skinned.

Using a large knife, make some deep scores diagonally into your chicken. Around 2 scores into each the thigh and 1 down the leg will do the trick. This will help your marinade to penetrate into the meat.

In a large mixing bowl add the grated ginger, and salt chilli powder, crushed garlic, tandoori masala, oil, yoghurt and mix this all around well. Your mixture will be a bright coral red colour and smell wonderfully pungent!

Dip all of your chicken pieces into the tandoori mix and make sure that all parts have been well coated. Cover the bowl and refrigerate this overnight.

The next day, preheat your oven to gas mark 200. Lay your chicken evenly onto a foil lined baking tray and allow this to cook on a high heat 25 minutes. At this point take a peek at your chicken and turn all of the pieces over. Allow to cook for another 20 minutes. Your chicken will be cooked to perfection when you poke it with a skewer or knife and notice clear liquid leaving the meat.

Remove the chicken from the baking tray, sprinkle with the chopped coriander and a few squeezes of the lemon.

This dish can be served with some simple rice and a cucumber raita. It looks so fancy and tastes so good that no one will ever imagine how simple it is to cook.

Lamb Curry

This rich and dark curry is very fragrant with a slightly sweet taste. It is my nephew Maxi's favourite curry.

Ingredients:

- 1lb of diced lamb with or without bone. Trim off as much fat as you can.
- 1 onion, diced
- 3 cloves of garlic, crushed and chopped finely
- 1 inch cube of ginger, grated
- 1 teaspoonful of salt
- 1/2 can of tinned tomatoes
- 1 tablespoonful of curry powder
- 1 teaspoonful of turmeric powder
- 1 stick of cinnamon
- 1 teaspoonful of jeera powder (this is the Mauritian name for cumin)
- A few sprigs of chopped coriander
- 1 medium potato - diced
- 1/2 cup of frozen peas. These will add a lovely texture to this dish.

Method:

First you need to warm your lamb which helps release a lot of the fat. Under a medium flame warm a non stick frying pan. When the pan is warmed up, add the lamb and let it cook gently for 5 minutes, stirring it around once or twice. The lamb will change colour from dark red to a pale grey brown colour and there will be a lot of liquid released.

Taking care to not spill the meat everywhere, pour out the liquid from the cooking lamb and drain this into a bowl. Once it's cooled down this liquid will solidify. Scoop out this fat and discard in the bin.

Now take out a heavy bottomed pan. Add a spoonful of oil and heat over a medium flame. When the oil has heated up add your onions and allow these to soften for 1-2 minutes.

Next add the warmed lamb and the diced potato and let this fry together for 5 minutes, stirring occasionally.

Add your cinnamon stick, jeera, turmeric and curry powder, ginger, and garlic and mix these ingredients carefully together. Stir for a couple of minutes to make sure that everything has combined thoroughly.

Now add 1/2 cup of water, sprinkle in the salt and stir everything again to make sure that none of the dry spices are stuck to the bottom of the pan. Now bring this to the boil.

When the curry has come to the boil cover the pan, lower the heat to a very low flame, cover the pan with a lid and allow this to simmer, the spices to absorb. Simmer away for 20 minutes.

Now, add your tomatoes and the frozen peas, stir them all around, cover your pan again and allow to cook for another 10 - 15 minutes. You will know when it is ready when your sauce has thickened slightly and taken on a rich brown colour.

To finish off sprinkle with the chopped coriander and inhale the gorgeous aroma.

Eat with a stack of puris or some plain rice. It's rather fabulous with faratha.

DELICIOUS MAURITIUS

Lamb Daube

Pronounced lamb dob

Lamb daube is perfect for someone who doesn't like the spiciness or the heaviness of curry. This recipe results in a more tangy and less chilli-hot dish with nuggets of lamb swimming in a glorious tomatoey sauce. It smells sensational.

Ingredients:

- 1/4 lb of lamb, diced with or without bone. (I prefer without bone because I have cracked a number of teeth on hidden lamb bones, however lamb bones do add extra richness to the finished product so it is a bit of a dilemma…)
- 2 medium sized onions finely chopped
- 4 cloves of garlic, crushed and chopped
- A couple of sprigs of thyme
- 2 chillis, chopped or sliced lengthways
- A cube of ginger, roughly 1 inch square, finely grated
- Salt to taste
- 2 tablespoons of vegetable oil
- 4 tomatoes cut up roughly

Method:

Add the diced lamb to a wok or sturdy frying pan - as it is a fatty meat you don't need to add any additional oil to the pan. Gently warm the lamb over a medium flame and stir it round from time to time to make sure that the it doesn't stick. Cook in this way for around 5 minutes.

You will notice that some liquid will drain from the meat. Taking care to not spill your cooking meat, carefully drain this away into a bowl or plate, allow to cool and discard. Don't pour this down the sink or it will create a fatberg that will be impossible to shift.

Continue cooking the drained meat until it becomes slightly browned. Now add the oil and the onions to the warmed lamb and fry it over a medium heat for another 5 minutes, mixing from time to time.

Add the tomato, garlic, chilli ginger thyme and salt. Mix everything together, cover and let it cook slowly slowly (my mum's words) over a medium flame for a further five minutes. Finally, reduce the heat to a low flame and cook for 10 more minutes until the tomato has softened beautifully.

Chicken Curry

The Twin Cockerels

When I was 10 my mum and I went to visit a psychic who worked out of a dimly lit room filled with smoke and glinting treasures. She didn't use palmistry or astrological charts for her soothsaying but instead was able to glimpse into our futures by rattling peacock feathers over our heads.

As we were about to leave the psychic's house my mother spied twin cockerels scratching about in the yard. Proud and glossy with sleek black plumage. She bought them and they travelled home with us in the car, their feathers peeking out of a basket we procured from somewhere.

Swiftly dispatched upon our return home, they re emerged as dinner in the form of a creamy chicken curry. I can't quite recall how it tasted - I was probably still quivering over those astonishing peacock feathers.

This recipe for chicken curry has a lovely thick sauce - enriched simply by adding a potato!

Ingredients:

- 1 packet of skinned chicken legs or thighs, roughly 8 pieces of chicken which will feed 4 people
- 1 big onion chopped
- 4 cloves of garlic crushed and chopped
- 1/2 tin of tomato
- 2 tablespoonfuls of curry powder

- 1 tablespoonful of turmeric
- 1 inch cube of ginger, grated
- 1 teaspoonful of salt
- 1/2 cup frozen peas
- 1 cup of water
- 1 medium potato, cut into tiny cubes
- 4 tablespoonfuls of plain yoghurt

Method:

Heat 2 tablespoonfuls of vegetable oil in a medium sized pan and gently fry the chicken, add the chopped potato and stir regularly over a medium flame. You want the chicken to turn a light brown colour. My mum says that if you skip this step, no longer how long you cook your curry, the finished product will not taste quite done. So fry the chicken for about 5 minutes, ok?

Now, add the onions to the chicken and cook together for another couple of minutes until the onions have softened.

Now add the curry powder, turmeric, garlic and ginger. Stir this around and fry this for another 2-3 minutes. Sprinkle on the salt. Now add the tomato and let this cook for another 2 - 3 minutes.

Next, add a cup of water to the curry mixture, turn up the heat and bring it to the boil. This will take about 5 minutes. When everything is bubbling away nicely, turn the heat to low, add the frozen peas, cover with a lid and let it simmer for 1/2 hour.

At the end of the cooking period, add some chopped coriander, sir in the yoghurt at the last possible moment, breathe in the delicious aroma and serve it immediately with some plain rice.

Vijay

Vijay was a glamorous man with a golden tooth and a glint of danger. He loved to go hunting in the Domaine du Chasseur, driven to this wilderness by his chauffeur "It's pronounced Chauffeuuuur, not Chofa!".

He would prepare the spoils of these hunting trips himself, skinning and disembowelling the game in his garage, cigarette dangling from lips and then prepare us succulent meals with the meat. Seared with flavour they were.

When Vijay came to England for his final tour, he bought strips of crispy pork belly from Chinatown and crunched them right out of the bag.

Venison curry

Venison curry is cooked without water. It is a curry that could easily pass as a pickle. In any case it is extremely flavoursome and is perfect for a special occasion.

Ingredients:

- 1 lb of venison chopped into inch size cubes
- 2 tablespoonful of ground cumin
- 1 tablespoonful of curry powder
- 1 teaspoonful of turmeric powder
- 1 stick of cinnamon
- 2 cups of red wine or cooking sherry.
- 1 chilli
- 1 inch of ginger, grated finely
- 3 cloves of garlic, crushed and chopped
- 1 teaspoonful of salt
- 3 tablespoonful of vegetable oil
- 4 tomatoes, or 1 tin of tomatoes

Method:

Under a medium flame bring your wine to the boil. When it is boiling set a light to it. This will burn off the alcohol. You will then be left with the lovely rich flavour but without the alcohol. Set this aside.

Heat the oil in a heavy bottomed pan or wok and when hot add the onions and allow to fry under a medium flame for 2 minutes until they are soft and translucent.

Now add the venison to the onions and fry for 5 minutes stirring gently.

Add your ground cumin, curry powder, turmeric ginger and garlic and stir this together for 3 minutes.

Add the cinnamon stick now and the boiled wine, lower the heat to a low flame and let it simmer covered for 1/2 hour.

At the end of this time stir everything nicely, add your tomatoes, stir again, put the lid back on and allow to simmer again under a very low flame for another 10 minutes. If you cook it on too high a flame you run the risk of drying out the venison.

This recipe will serve 4 - 5 people. It is best served with rice, dal and a simple salad.

Pickles

When returning from Mauritius, my family love nothing more than to bring home large slightly sticky jars of home made pickles, the less hermetically sealed the better. Starting at take off, chilli and garlic infused oil will start to slowly leak from their glass pickling jar. During the long flight back to London this glistening and golden oil will soak profusely through carefully stowed bundles of clothes and packets of Mauritian tea, suffusing all with the sweet smell of turmeric and oil.

Most people love to have a couple of pickles on the side. I can gleefully eat a plateful of pickles in one sitting.

- Mango Koucha
- Fish Vindaye
- Vegetable Pickle
- Pineapple with Salt and Chilli

Mango Koucha*

Pronounced Mango Koo-cha
*This is how my mum imagines that it is spelled.

Here in England you can buy green mangoes from Indian shops only when they are in season - you certainly can't buy them every day. If you'd like to make this you will need to keep your eyes peeled for small green mangoes, about the size of an apple, that haven't developed much of a hard pip. When you cut one of these open and discover a little white pip, congratulations you have hit the green mango jackpot and can proceed to make this dainty dish.

You could eat this as an accompaniment to dal and a simple vegetable curry of some sort. I like to eat this on its own with a fork. As I write those words my mouth starts to water!

Ingredients:

- 1 lb of green mangoes, peeled
- A big tablespoonful of ground mustard (this is dry mustard powder, or you can roughly grind your own mustard seeds)
- 3 - 4 large hot chillis.
- 1 teaspoonful of turmeric
- 4 cloves of garlic
- 1 teaspoonful of salt (or to taste)
- A tablespoonful of tamarind. Make sure that you remove the stones.
- 2 tablespoonfuls sunflower or corn oil

Method:

Peel the green mango and discard the white pip in the middle. Now grate the mango. It needs to be quite rough so choose the grater accordingly. A standard cheese grater works well. After you have grated it then take the mango into your hands and squeeze it hard so that all of the liquid is extracted from it. Discard that liquid.

Now add all of the spices, the oil, salt and garlic and chilli in a bowl, add the mango and mix everything together. It will combine together better if you use your hands. Everything will turn yellow (including your hands!) and it will taste of tangy mustardy chilli heaven.

Put it into a plastic container and keep in the fridge.

This will keep for a whole month in a sealed container.

Fish Vindaye

Pronounced Fish Vind-eye

Fish Vindaye is a spicy fish pickle which tastes particularly good with some baguette and maybe a tiny bit of salad on the side. According to my mum this dish is not at all fattening and is therefore perfect for those watching their weight this means that you have have an extra bit without feeling remotely guilty. Fish Vindaye is a dish best served cold, right from the fridge or cool bag.

Ingredients:

- 1 lb of deboned fish cut into 1/2 inch slices. Tuna, red snapper or red mullet works well, oily fish like salmon or mackerel don't. In Mauritius you would make this with Spadon. Remove the skin or keep it on.
- 2 tablespoonfuls of mustard seeds
- 1 tablespoon of malt vinegar
- Salt to taste (roughly 1 teaspoonful)
- 1 heaped teaspoonful of turmeric powder
- 4 chillis (hot ones) halved lengthways
- 4 tablespoonfuls of vegetable cooking oil
- 6 smallish onions (about the size of shallots - or you can just use shallots instead of onions) cut these into quarters
- 4 cloves of garlic crushed and finely chopped
- Couple of tablespoonfuls of oil for frying the fish

Method:

You start by gently frying the fish in 2 tablespoonfuls of oil for around 2 minutes on each side. It doesn't need to be completely cooked - take it off just before it becomes crispy. The fish should feel soft and be slightly browned. Pop the fried fish aside on a plate. If you worry about eating raw fish, don't - the vinegar which you will add later on will finish the cooking process.

Add the mustard, turmeric, salt, chilli, vinegar and garlic and oil into a largish bowl and mix together thoroughly.

In a new frying pan, heat another spoonful of oil and fry the onions gently for 1 or 2 minutes. You don't want the onions going soft and brown, we want them to stay crunchy and a bit raw.

Now add the mustard and spice mix to your pan of warmed onions and mix everything together thoroughly.

Next we add the fish to the pan, pour over the vinegar evenly and carefully coat all of the fish with the spicy-sour-oily oniony mixture. Leave it all to cool down for a few minutes and then transfer to a plastic Tupperware tub - coating the spicy oil over everything as evenly as you can.

If at this point - heavens forbid - your Fish Vindaye looks a little bit dry all you need to do is to drizzle over a spoonful or more oil over it all. Leave to cool down to room temperature, replace the Tupperware lid and pop into the fridge.

When your Fish Vindaye has cooled down fully it is ready to eat. Refrigerated, this will keep well for about 2 weeks.

Vegetable Pickle

My mum's grandmother would make this pickle on particularly hot summer's days. She would lay the prepared vegetables out to dry in her garden, letting the summer sun work its magic on the raw ingredients. This rather crisp Vegetable Pickle has a fresh and intense mustard hot flavour. It is served cool and can be eaten either in a baguette or just on its own. When you eat dish this your mouth will water and your nose will start to decongest - a boon for those plagued with sinus problems.

Ingredients:

- 1/2 a small green cabbage (one of the hard ones, like a pale green bowling ball, not a dark green leafy one). This needs to be finely shredded either using a knife or a food processor.
- 2 medium sized carrots. Cut them lengthways into long thin strips roughly the size of half a fine green bean (if you were to split this bean along it's length)
- A handful of fine green beans. These need to be topped and tailed with the string removed. Then carefully slice them lengthways. This will take some time but they will look very elegant and it is worth the effort.
- 4 chillis. These are to be cut in half lengthways or chopped finely, whichever you prefer. I think it looks nicer lengthways and they are easier to fish out if you don't like your food too hot.
- 4 cloves of garlic, crushed and finely chopped
- 1 level tablespoonful of salt

- 2 tablespoonfuls of dry mustard seeds
- 1 teaspoonful of turmeric
- 1 tablespoonful of vinegar
- 3 tablespoonfuls of vegetable oil (not olive oil, use something with a lighter flavour like corn oil)

Method:

Using a grinder or pestle and mortar roughly grind up the mustard seeds. Set these beautifully ground seeds aside into a mixing bowl.

Now throw in the chilli, garlic, turmeric, salt, oil and vinegar to the ground mustard seeds and mix everything together.

Half fill a big pan with water and bring this to the boil. The pan will need to be big enough to hold all of the vegetables that you have chopped up.

When the water is boiling, add the cabbage, carrots and beans to the boiling water. Let the vegetables boil for one minute. Don't let them overcook - the aim is to blanch rather than to boil to mush. Remove the blanched vegetables from the water with a slotted spoon and set aside in a bowl until they are cool enough to handle by hand.

When the vegetables have cooled down, take up handfuls of the vegetables and squeeze them gently in order to remove any excess water. The aim of the game here is to remove both the water that they were blanched in as well as any excess water contained within the vegetables themselves.

Spread the vegetables out onto a plate or tray and cover with a tea towel and leave outside in the sun to dry out for 1/2 a day. Isn't that the most lovely cooking instruction you've ever read?

When your vegetables have been thoroughly sun kissed sprinkle the spice mix over the vegetables and mix everything together making sure that everything is well coated. Finally add your vegetable pickle to a plastic Tupperware box, cover with a lid and refrigerate. You can leave it there for up to 3 weeks. If you leave it there for too long your Tupperware will turn yellow - so best eat it quick.

My Dad who Planted Trees

Set back from the banks of a trickling river is a tiny blue tent in which a little boy lives with his parents. Cross the river carefully and in a few minutes time you will come across Camp La Boue.

Around 20 years ago or so, my my dad planted a field of small saplings in this scrap of land. Every time he visited Mauritius, which was every five years or so, he would visit the young trees and clear away tangles of weeds and brambles, and squirt some fertiliser here and there.

If you were to visit Camp La Boue at the right time of year you today will be rewarded by an orchard of established lychee trees that yield sprays of large soft fruit, blushing pink when ripe. Did you know that is how lychees grow? Like bunches of plumptious flowers they are. Warmed by the sun they taste fantastic.

Pineapple with Salt and Chilli

Although this is a very simple and quick recipe it is very flavoursome! At seasides and in the middle of the city you will find people selling plastic bags of this for a couple of Mauritian rupees each. Spicy and sweet this is an unusual way of eating perfectly ripe pineapples. If you like you can substitute the pineapple with mango. This tastes awfully good as well.

Ingredients:

- 1 pineapple, peeled and chopped however you wish
- 2 chillis chopped finely
- Sprinkle of salt to taste

Method:

Add your pineapple to a Tupperware box and sprinkle with salt. Close the lid and shake well. Now, add your chilli and close the box and shake well again. Leave it for a minute or so and shake again so that all of the juices soak up the spice

Eat!

Soups and Dals

From clear bouillons to rich and creamy channa dal, Mauritius has a wide variety of soups and dals that are perfect either as side dishes or can stand alone as the main event. Mauritians like my mum will generally splash dal onto the side of their plate and will mush everything together with their fingers. A thinner soup or bouillon will generally be served with a bowl and spoon.

- Bouillon
- Black Dal
- Dal Pitta
- Channa Dal
- Dynorod Soup
- Crab Soup
- Saffron

Bouillon

Pronounced Boo-yon

This is a delicate, clear and light soup. The Chinese Cabbage has a lovely fresh flavour and is perfect if you feel in need of a cleansing day. You can eat this dish if you want to lose a bit of weight - the broth is filling but contains pretty much zero calories.

You can substitute a couple of handfuls of watercress instead of the Chinese Cabbage. The watercress version has a slightly more peppery flavour.

This recipe will serve 4 people

Ingredients:

- 1 Chinese cabbage chopped into cubes roughly 2 inches long
- 1 cube of ginger, grated
- 2 cloves of garlic, grated
- 1/4 of a big onion, finely chopped
- 2 tablespoonfuls of vegetable oil
- 1 little tomato, chopped
- 2 cups of water
- Salt to taste

Method:

First fry your onions in the oil. The flame needs to be a medium flame. Stir them around until they are a lovely golden colour.

Add the Chinese leaves and fry them for about 5 minutes. Keep stirring this so that nothing sticks.

At the end of the 5 minutes add the salt, garlic, and ginger and tomato and allow this to fry together for 2 more minutes.

Add the water. Bring everything to the boil for 5 minutes and let it bubble, bubble, bubble.

Lower the flame to very low, cover the pan and allow to simmer for a further 5 minutes.

At the end of the cooking time you will be left with a lovely flavoursome soup which smells delicious.

Black Dal

Pronounced Black Dal (not Dahl)

Black lentil or green lentil dal is one of my favourite things to eat after a cold day on the mean streets of South London. A hefty mug of this lovely soup is so warming and extremely comforting. If you live in a sunnier clime and don't need a winter warmer add a bit more water to this at the end of the cooking time.

You can eat this dish on its own, or as a side dish to pretty much any main dish. My favourite way is to eat it with some scrumptious fried potatoes, a faratha and perhaps some tomato chutney. Heavenly!

Ingredients:

- 1/2 medium sized onion, either chopped or sliced lengthwise around 1 cm in width
- 2 cloves of garlic crushed and chopped
- 2 medium sized tomatoes
- Sprig of thyme plucked from the garden
- Salt to taste
- 2 tablespoonfuls of vegetable oil
- 1 cup of dry black lentils that have been previously soaked in cold water overnight.

Method:

You can make this in a pressure cooker or in a pan. A pressure cooker will take much less time to cook so if you have one best dig it out.

Drain the soaking water away from the lentils and give them a rinse. Drain away the excess water. Pour the lentils into your pressure cooker, add 4 cups of water and sprinkle in the salt. Securely seal the lid of your pressure cooker shut according to the instructions, pop the little whistling thing atop and bring to the boil (you'll know that this has happened once the steam starts to whoosh out of the top) and allow to boil for a further 5 minutes.

If you don't have a pressure cooker and are cooking in a pan it will take some time and is far less economical. You will need to cover your pan with a lid and boil away for about 40 minutes. Make sure that you check that the water doesn't dry out from time to time, and add more if necessary.

Whichever way you choose to cook your lentils, make sure that at the end of the cooking time they are sweet and tender.

Fry the onions separately in the oil until they are brown. Add the garlic, thyme and tomato to the onions and stir this gently over a low heat until everything is soft and cooked. Stir all the time.

Add the onion and tomato mixture to the lentils and stir it in.

Let everything cook together on a low heat, not under pressure, for about 5 minutes (so take off the pressure cooker whistle topper for this part). At the end of the cooking period give everything a final stir. If you like a thinner dal, you can add some water at this point.

Possible variation:

If you want you can add a handful of spinach to the dal at the end of the cooking period. This is very tasty as well as being a wonderful way to invisibly incorporate some greens into your evening meal. If you want to do this the only change you need to make to the recipe above is to add 1 teaspoonful of curry powder and 1 teaspoonful of turmeric powder when you are at the frying onion stage.

Dal Pitha

Pronounced Dal Pit-Tha

What is Dal Pitha? Small soft pastry squares afloat in a sea of black dal, softening and soaking up the flavour. My mum says that they used to eat this in Mauritius before pasta came to the island. A simple meal that's perfect for when you are feeling nostalgic or might be in need of a friendly hug. This is a profoundly warming, filling and satisfying meal.

Ingredients:

- 1 small cup of black lentils, washed
- 1 onion, finely chopped
- 1 teaspoonful of salt
- 1 teaspoonful of turmeric
- 3 tablespoonfuls of vegetable oil
- 1½ cups of white plain flour
- 1/4 cup of water (for the dough)
- 4 small cups of water (for your dal)

Method:

First you need to make the dough. Add ½ a tablespoonful of oil to your flour, and mix this up using your hands for a minute.

Now make a well in the centre of your flour and slowly add your water to the centre of the hole and work it together until you have made a medium soft dough. Knead this dough for 2-3 minutes and you will produce a soft dough. If it feels a bit too sticky keep on kneading it, it will be alright - I'm sure that there is a life lesson in there somewhere. If at the end of this kneading time it still looks a bit soft, put the dough into the fridge and this will sort it out. If all is looking well, cover and leave to rest on the side until you are ready for it.

Next put the lentils into a pressure cooker, add the water and salt. Put the lid on, bring to the boil (it will whistle at that point) reduce the heat to a medium flame and allow to cook for a further 10 minutes. Remove from the heat. When it's safe to do so, check to see if the lentils are nice and soft. If they are not yet cooked, boil it again with the lid on for another 5 minutes. When cooked, remove from the heat and sprinkle with the turmeric. Stir well.

Let's now return to the dough. Take out your rolling pin and board. Lightly dust both with flour and roll out the dough until it is very thin, about as thick as a sheet of lasagne, about 1mm thick. Cut this out into squares of 1 1/2 inch.

We are now going to put everything together. Return your dal to a low heat. Little by little, add your pastry squares to the dal and stir these in gently taking care to not to break them up. Do this until you have added them all. Please don't add them all in one go or you will be left with a mass of uncooked dough, instead take your time and enjoy the process: A second life lesson hidden in a recipe for Dal Pitha!

Allow this to simmer over a low heat, for 10 - 15 minutes until everything has thickened and the Dal Pitha has absorbed some of the water and become nice and soft. Meanwhile, put your onion to fry over a medium flame. Fry these for 5 minutes or so until they are golden, but not crisp. When they have reached this sweet point add the onions to the dal pita and stir them in lovingly.

Remove from the heat and serve in a bowl. I enjoy eating this just as it is. It's such a perfect meal if you are feeling a little under the weather and in need of succour.

DELICIOUS MAURITIUS

Channa Dal

Pronounced Chan-Na Dal

Channa dal is one of the most comforting dishes that you can make and after a bowl of this you will feel replete and content. This ochre yellow soup is surprisingly low in calories, making this recipe a close confidant to those trying to quietly shift a couple of pounds. Its colour comes from the pale yellow of the channa dal itself which is further intensified by the sprinkle of turmeric powder.

You can eat this dal on its own or as an ideal accompaniment to rice dishes and curries of all sorts. Serve it either ladled directly onto your plate (as a Mauritian born would do) or large mug (as a London born Mauritian like me would do).

Ingredients:

- 1 medium cup of channa dal. This needs to be soaked overnight if you are using dry dal. Once it has been soaked, discard the soaking water. If you are using a pressure cooker then you can skip this overnight soaking - so another reason for you to invest in one.
- 1/2 a large onion, diced
- 2-3 cloves of garlic, crushed and chopped
- 1 tablespoonful of whole cumin seeds
- 1 tablespoonful of curry powder
- 1 teaspoonful of turmeric powder
- 1 teaspoonful of salt
- 2 tomatoes, chopped
- A few sprigs of coriander

- 2 tablespoonfuls of vegetable oil
- 1 small potato, peeled and sliced into small chunks.
- A few curry leaves (optional but tasty). You can find these in Indian or Chinese shops.

Method:

Cook the dal in 2 cups of water until they have become soft and fluffy.

If you use a regular pan to cook your dal this will take around 30 - 40 minutes. Bring to the boil on a high flame then cover and reduce the heat to medium for the rest of the cooking time.

If you intend to use a pressure cooker bring the dal and the water to boil on a high flame until the steam comes whistling out of the top. This will take around 5 minutes. Then lower the flame and heat on a low flame for about 10 - 15 minutes.

When the dal is cooked it will be nice and soft in texture. At this point turn the heat off and set aside. Don't drain away the cooking liquid - this will add to the tastiness and glossy nature of the finished soup.

Whilst your dal is busily boiling away now is the time to make a start on preparing the rest of the ingredients. Fry the onions and cumin seeds in the oil over a medium flame until they are lightly browned and soft - this will take about a minute or so. As you don't want the onions to become too crispy or the cumin seeds to stick and burn, please remember to stir everything around occasionally.

Add the garlic, curry powder, and turmeric powder to this mixture and then add 2 tablespoonfuls of water. Give everything a good mix at this point to make sure that nothing gets stuck to the bottom of the pan. Let this mixture cook for 1 minute over a medium flame. Now add the chopped potato and chopped tomatoes and stir these around. Sprinkle with salt to taste. Lower the flame and let this cook

DELICIOUS MAURITIUS

on a low flame until the tomatoes are nice and soft this will take around 5 minutes or so. At the end of this time you will have made a lovely yellowy light brown paste, one that will smell heavenly.

Now let's put everything together. Take your heavenly paste and then add this to the dal. Stir everything well and cook uncovered over a low flame for about 10 minutes. (If you discover that your dal is not soft enough, cook it with the lid on and it will become nice and soft)

One minute before you are ready to eat sprinkle in the chopped coriander leaves. Serve piping hot.

Dynorod Soup

Jewish chicken soup in disguise

At the beginning of the year my mum tripped over and needed an operation to knit together a fractured patella (that's your knee bone). The general anaesthetic entirely knocked her for six. She lost all desire to eat or drink and found it impossible to keep anything down. This played havoc with her various rhythms which further…compacted the problem. I made this soup for her and a) it was the first meal that she found tasty and b) it appears to have had remarkable…scouring powers.

Dynorod soup is tasty and filled with the essence of good things.

Ingredients:

- A large chicken (free range or organic if you can). No giblets.
- 2 large carrots, cut into 2
- 1 onion, cut into 2
- 5 cloves of garlic, rinsed
- A bunch of parsley, rinsed
- 2 sticks of celery cut into 2
- Salt to taste
- A couple of chicken stock cubes
- Water

DELICIOUS MAURITIUS

Method:

You will need to have a big pan. It won't work in a normal sized pan as the chicken wont fit and everything will bubble over and you will have a big mess to clean. A huge pan is mandatory.

Put your chicken into this pan, add the carrots, onion, garlic parsley and celery and then cover the whole lot with water until everything is covered.

Now bring it to the boil and let is all boil and bubble for 30 minutes. A frankly appalling scum will rise up to the top. Using a big spoon and being careful not to remove too much of the water, scrape off and discard this scum. Its harmless and probably filled with goodness but it looks unappetising and so it's got to go.

Reduce the heat now and cover it up and let it simmer for hours. Around 3 hours of simmering. It is a long process, but you are essentially imbuing the cooking liquid with all of the goodness from the chicken from its skin to its bones. This will nourish you deeply. After hour 1 your entire home will smell of boiling chicken, the kitchen windows will start to sweat - yet still you need to keep boiling!

After 3 hours have gone by, carefully remove the chicken from the watery stock and place in a cooking bowl. When its cool enough to handle, pick off most of the chicken from the bones and set this aside. Put the rest of the carcass back into the pan together with any stock that has escaped. Add one or two chicken stock cubes and some salt (not too much - remember that this stock will reduce) at this point and allow to simmer again for another 2 hours.

Fish out the chicken carcass, onion, garlic, and discard - their work here is done. Return a few chunks of the boiled chicken and carrot to the pan, et voila!

Will the smell of boiled chicken ever rinse out of your hair, clothes and carpet? This is doubtful. Is it worth the time it takes to cook? Undoubtably. Enjoy your shimmering elixir piping hot with a bit of the carrot and a few shreds of the chicken. If you fancy, you could throw in a couple of strands of cooked spaghetti, but nothing else is needed.

Dinorod soup will keep happily in the fridge for a few days, setting to a jelly. If you are counting calories you could scrape off its flabby top layer. I prefer to eat it all up as nature intended - your skin and hair will thank you for it - and your large intestine will relax and breathe a sigh of relief.

Crab Soup

I associate crab soup with early mornings when I was little and sleepy drives through London to the Billingsgate Fish Market. Bundled up tight in duffle coat and wellies I would toddle amazed through slush and bustle, fishy smells and scales. We'd be home by 9am, warming our cockles with a bowl of this soon afterwards.

If you have a slightly stuffy nose or a lingering cold, a bowl of this crab soup will work wonders. Not only will it remove the chestiness from your throat and clear out your pipes but all the fun of poking out your delicious crab meat will help you forget your malaise. This recipe calls for a whole crab that we will proceed to cook in a spicy gingery broth.

If you feel light headed at the thought of consigning a live crab to its scrabbling doom - don't fret. A whole ready cooked crab will still taste heavenly. You can also ask your fishmonger to clean and prepare a pre-boiled one. Use all of it up to make this dish. A crab's hairy legs are delicious!

This recipe will serve 4

Ingredients:

- 1 large boiled crab, get this prepared by your fishmonger or cook it yourself. It needs to be cleaned, with the claws and legs removed and cracked. Split the shell into 4 parts. This makes it easier to eat and also allows it's fishy juices out.
- 1 stock cube - chicken, fish or vegetable are all fine
- 1 onion chopped into cubes

- 3 cloves of garlic, crushed
- 1 inch cube of ginger, peeled and grated finely
- 1 sprig of thyme
- 2 whole hot chillis
- 2 tomatoes, chopped roughly
- 1 teaspoonful of salt
- 1/4 teaspoonful of ground mustard powder. If you have whole mustard, just grind this up
- 2 tablespoonfuls of vegetable oil
- 1 tablespoonful of curry powder
- 1/4 teaspoonful of ground black pepper
- 2 pints of water

Method:

Put your onion, garlic, ginger, chilli, tomato and thyme into a blender and blend these all together until they are a soft paste. Set this aside.

In a large cooking pot heat your oil over a medium flame. When the oil is hot, put in your crab pieces and stir this around. Now add your ground pepper, salt, curry powder and mustard and stir this around again. Reduce the heat to low and stir this and allow to cook covered for 5 minutes. Peep every now and them to make sure that it is not sticking. If it starts to stick add a splash of water to calm things down.

Now add the ingredients from your blender. Mix this all together, cover, then allow to cook gently for another five minutes keeping your temperature low. This will start to sizzle, it will smell aromatic with the piquancy that only ginger and garlic and crab can.

Now, raise the heat to high. Add the rest of your water (you might like to rinse out your blender with this water to make sure that you have used all of your lovely spice mixture) and crumble in your stock cube. Cover it up again and bring this to a bubbling boil. Let this boil on high for 5 minutes.

Now, reduce the heat to low again and let this simmer for 10 - 15 minutes. Its now ready!

Ladle this soup steaming hot into your bowls and dive in. I would just eat it as it is, bread doesn't really go with a soup like this.

Have a plate on the side - a Poubelle de Table if you fancy being fancy - for the crab shells.

A stash of sturdy tissues (into which you can blow your streaming nose) will also come in handy.

Saffron

Pronounced Saf-Ron (you need to roll the r in the back of your throat)

Although this obviously isn't a soup it is marvellous at shifting colds, snuffles and the like - apparently it is an ancient Ayurvedic tonic. My mum would make us drink this whenever we had a sore throat - and it always worked! Apparently there is some chemical reaction that takes place when black pepper is cooked in warm milk. Not all of my mum's home cures were as effective: Her remedy for coldsores involved lighting an oily wick and rolling it over the affected lip. It usually resulted in a blackened, burnt, and slightly more sore lip. So we will steer clear of that one for now.

This drink has an earthy and filling taste and it good for when you are feeling out of sorts. One final thing - if you plan to take any selfies with your tongue sticking out, please take 'em before drinking this as it will stain your tongue a bright sunshine yellow and will remain like that for quite a while.

Ingredients:

- 1 mug of milk
- 1 tablespoonful of turmeric powder
- Honey to taste (a tablespoonful or so will be perfect)
- A few grinds of black pepper

Method:

Pour the milk and turmeric into a milk pan and heat up slowly. Don't leave it alone as you don't want it to boil over. Add a few

DELICIOUS MAURITIUS

grinds of black pepper. If you don't have whole peppercorns, a couple of pinches of pre-ground pepper will do just as well.

Just before it boils, remove from the stove and pour into a mug, add the honey to taste and sip it whilst it's hot.

You'll feel better soon.

Fire

If you are Mauritian man, or married to a Mauritian woman, it is likely that you will have been invited to partake of an evening of Fire.

Fire is loosely translated as sitting around and drinking solidly for hours. Whiskey or rum are the liquors of choice. Downed neat, or with a splash of Coca Cola - or soda water if you are looking after your health. Fire ain't for the faint hearted: my strapping brother in law was not able to keep up and had to bow out with liquid grace - probably under my sister's steely gaze.

I think I have done Fire once. I'm not entirely sure.

Seafood

Mauritius is a tiny island located off the coast of South Africa. If you continue past Madagascar and keep on going into the heart of the Indian Ocean you'll eventually arrive at it. The island is fringed with coral reefs that teem with fish. So it's no surprise that there are a plethora of Mauritian seafood recipes.

- Gigantic Grilled King Prawns
- Mauritian Fish Curry
- Prawn Curry
- Sardine and Tomato Salad
- Octopus Curry
- Octopus Cooked in the Pickling Style
- Din's recipe for Octopus Curry

Gigantic Grilled King Prawns

If you have a lot of people to feed you are going to have to come to terms with the fact that you are going to have a very gross morning cleaning and gutting these delicacies. Once you have inhaled and exhaled and come to terms with this let us make a start. I promise you that it is absolutely worth it in the end.

These prawns are exceptionally succulent, sweet and delicious. The grey, green prawns curl up over the heat and turn a coral peach colour that shows that they are done.

To prepare your prawns ready to cook you will need:

- A strong stomach
- A bowl in which to hold the prawns
- Another bowl for discarded bits
- A small sharp knife
- Water to rinse

How to prepare these prawns:

Pick up your gorgeous dangling prawn by its middle. Around half way up you will notice where the head attaches to the body. Nod the prawn's head forward and pop the tip of your knife into the bit that opens up. Now, setting aside all squeamishness you must squeeze on either side of the nick that you have made. A foul goop that looks a little bit like the inside of a passion fruit will well up. Squeeze this mess into your bowl.

DELICIOUS MAURITIUS

Next, cut along the centre of the prawn's back. You will see a black line running along here. This is poo. Unless you are a copraphage you must now pull this out. It will come out quite easily. Rinse the whole prawn and thank heavens that you are now done. Try to keep the heads and legs on and as intact as possible as not only do they look great but they are delicious to crunch and chew on - but not to eat though.

Finish cleaning all of your prawns and pop into the fridge until you are ready to cook them later that day.

Ingredients:

- 1 kilo of gigantic prawns
- 3 cloves of garlic, crushed
- Salt to taste
- Freshly ground pepper
- 2 chillis, sliced lengthways
- Couple of spoonfuls of vegetable oil
- Sprigs of thyme
- For garnish
- 2 lemons
- 2 spring onions, chopped finely

Method:

Mix up all of your ingredients and allow these to marinade for an hour or so before you want to eat.

First, heat your frying pan or griddle pan until it is very hot. Lay as many marinated prawns as you can onto your frying pan. If you have an extractor fan now is the time to switch it on or open a window as the heated chillis can make the air a bit chokey.

The prawns will change colour to a bright orangey pink when they are done.

I like to sprinkle them with some lemon juice whilst it cooks. It looks very festive and the smell is divine. Let the edges of the prawns singe a bit and don't remove from the heat too soon - let everything crisp up. Total cooking time per batch is around 10 minutes, you can cook them for longer if you turn the heat a bit lower mid way.

To serve arrange in a big bowl, sprinkle with the spring onion and finish with final squeeze of lemon.

Divine!

Mauritian Fish Curry

Everyone in Mauritius loves fish curry and it is often served on special occasions. When I visited Mauritius for the first time in 15 years I was served this fish curry by every relative that I went to visit. This particularly scrummy version comes in a light and delicately spiced sauce.

Ingredients:

- 1 lb of fresh fish like snapper, grey or red mullet work particularly well. This needs to be prepared and sliced into 3/4 inch width portions. Keep the head, tail and don't remove the skin. You will have around 5 slices per fish.
- 1 medium sized onion, sliced or diced. I prefer it when they are thinly sliced as it just feels more authentic.
- 3 cloves of garlic, crushed and finely chopped
- 1 inch of ginger, grated finely
- 2 tablespoonfuls of curry powder
- 1 teaspoonful of turmeric powder
- 3 tablespoonfuls of vegetable oil to fry the fish
- 2 tablespoonful of vegetable oil for the curry
- 1/2 tin of tomatoes
- 5 curry leaves
- 1 teaspoonful of salt, or to taste
- 1/4 bunch of coriander chopped finely as a garnish

Method:

First, lightly sprinkle the fish with salt.

Heat the oil in a large heavyish frying pan over a medium heat. When the oil is hot carefully add the slices of fish. If the pan is big enough, you will be able to get all 5 slices into the hot oil. Fry for 5 minutes, then using a fish slice turn them over carefully and allow to sizzle away for another 5 minutes. The fish will turn a lovely light brown colour. It doesn't need to go too crispy. Remove the fish from the oil and set this aside on a plate.

Now, discard the fish cooking oil and clean out the pan. When it is dry add 2 tablespoonfuls of fresh vegetable cooking oil and heat this over a medium flame until it is hot.

Add your sliced or diced onions to the oil and stir occasionally. Cook them for 2- 3 minutes until they have become luscious, golden brown and translucent. Now add the curry powder, turmeric, garlic and ginger. Continue to cook over a medium flame for another 2- 3 minutes, stirring well all the while. It it looks like things are starting to stick, getting a bit too dry for comfort and might start to burn, calm everything down by adding a splash or two of water.

Add the tomatoes and curry leaves now and stir together until it is all mixed up nicely. Next add a small cup of water turn up the heat to high and bring this curry sauce to the boil. At this point turn the heat back down to medium and allow to bubble away for another 5 minutes or so. You will be rewarded with a richly coloured subtly piquant sauce, a gravy with a medium-light consistency.

Now, taking care to not break up your slices, add the fish to your gorgeous sauce. Spoon the sauce over the fish so that every slice is completely covered and cook this uncovered on a medium flame for 5 minutes. Then cover the fish curry with a lid and allow to simmer on a low heat for a final 5 minutes.

DELICIOUS MAURITIUS

At the end of the cooking time, remove the lid, inhale the aroma and finally sprinkle on the chopped coriander. Your fish curry is ready to go.

You can enjoy this with rice, faratha, puree, or best of all with a stack of dal puris.

Les Quatre Bandes

The Mauritian Flag celebrates the vibrant natural and emotional technicolour that permeates the island. Les Quatre Bandes - The Four Bands - was adopted by Mauritius upon its independence in 1968 and represents both the beauty of the island and the spirit of independence of its people.

Red represents its struggle for freedom.

Blue represents the intensity of the Indian Ocean, upon which Mauritius floats.

Yellow represents the shining light of independence - remember that it was on this island that paid labour replaced slavery

Green represents the agriculture of Mauritius and how verdant it remains all year round

Isn't that beautiful?

Prawn Curry

Prawn curry is one of my favourite things to eat. Everything from the sweet prawns to the soft potato are so very satisfying. This is perfect with plain rice, or a softly puffed Naan bread. You don't need anything else on the side.

This recipe will serve 4 people

Ingredients:

- 1 kilo - about 30 - fresh king prawns, shell on, cleaned
- 1 big onion, chopped
- 4 cloves of garlic, crushed and finely chopped
- 1 inch cube of ginger, peeled and grated
- 2 tablespoonfuls of curry powder
- 1/2 can of tinned tomatoes
- 2 tablespoonfuls of oil
- 1 large potato, peeled and cubed
- 1 cup of frozen peas
- 1/2 teaspoonful of cumin powder
- 1/2 cup of water - 187ml
- 2 teaspoonful of salt
- 1/2 teaspoonful of turmeric powder
- A few curry leaves (optional)
- 1/2 bunch of finely chopped coriander leaves

Method:

Sprinkle 1 teaspoonful of your salt over the deveined and cleaned king prawns (see the recipe for Gigantic King Prawns to find out how to do this) Mix it all well. Heat up half of your oil in a wok. When the oil is hot, add around half of the prawns to cook. Let them fry for 2 minutes turning them over occasionally. The prawns will change colour to a charming coral pink colour. Remove from the oil and set aside and repeat with the other batch of prawns.

Wash and dry your wok, and add the rest of your oil. Heat this and then add the onions, and allow to fry for a minute or so. Next add the potato and fry them together until the onion has browned.

Now add the curry, cumin and turmeric powder, add 1/2 cup of water, and stir this around thoroughly. Stir this for 1 minute. Now add the tomato, garlic and ginger. Reduce the heat to low, cover and allow to simmer for 10 minutes.

By now the sauce will have thickened. Add the peas and now add the prawns. Sprinkle over the remaining salt and curry leaves. Give this a nice stir and make sure that everything is well coated. If you like a saucy curry now if the time to add another 1/4 cup of water. Cover again and let it simmer slowly slowly for 15 - 20 minutes.

Just before serving, sprinkle the whole lot with your chopped coriander leaves.

DELICIOUS MAURITIUS

Sardine and Tomato Salad

This salad is rather pretty with its bright red tomatoes and crisp white onion all mashed up with silvery sardines. It an ideal picnic lunch for a summer's day - it's so lovely to scoop this up with some crunchy bread. This recipe will serve 2 very nicely for lunch. Bring along this salad in a Tupperware and make your sandwiches up when you are ready to eat. You risk sogginess if you make it too far ahead.

Ingredients:

- 1 tin of sardines - in brine or oil, it is your choice
- 2 ripe tomatoes, chopped
- Sprinkle of salt to taste
- 1 small chilli, finely chopped
- 1 small onion, shallot size, finely chopped

Method:

This is a tough one. Drain the sardines and add them to a bowl. Add the rest of the ingredients. Mix together using a fork, mashing up all of the sardines into the tomatoes well.

Octopus Curry

I used to have an illustrated children's encyclopaedia that I loved to read curled up on a chair in the sewing room so called because my mum had her sewing machine in there. The letter O was illustrated with a vividly coloured picture of a gigantic octopus coming to get me with its eight swirling tentacles. Whenever I reached that awful page I would hurl the book to the other side of the sewing room in abject terror. Those eyes! Those beastly suckers!

When I was little I HATED octopus curry all because of that page and I would eat it slowly and spitefully. Now that I am far more sensible I adore eating octopus curry.

You don't use very much water in this dish and the intense sauce clings tightly to the octopus bits. It takes quite a bit of time to cook this as octopus needs to be very tender. It is worth the wait - A taste of the heavenly Indian Ocean in a fishy avatar.

Ingredients:

- 1 cleaned octopus, 5lb in weight
- 3 medium onions, finely chopped
- 1 can of tomatoes
- 3 spoonfuls of curry powder
- 1 teaspoonful of turmeric
- 1 teaspoonful cumin powder
- 5 cloves of garlic, crushed and chopped
- 1 inch cube of ginger, grated finely
- 1/4 bunch of coriander to garnish
- 3 - 4 tablespoonfuls of vegetable oil

DELICIOUS MAURITIUS

Method:

Take a big whole octopus . Your fishmonger will need to clean it for you as you don't want the head and you *certainly* don't want those eyes peering at you!

Octopus needs to be boiled and then boiled some more as it is quite a tough *fruit de mer* otherwise. Let is start by putting it into a pan of boiling water. Please don't add any salt as the octopus is already salty enough. Cover and bring this to the boil at which point reduce the heat to low and let it simmer for 1/2 hour.

At the end of 1/2 hour check to see if it has become tender. If not, then boil for another 10 minutes or so.

Remove from water and carefully chop up the octopus into bite sized pieces of approximately 1/2 inch. Set this aside now.

Take your heaviest cooking pot and add the oil. Heat this over a medium flame until the oil has heated up. Add the chopped onions and octopus at the same time and allow these to fry together for about 2 minutes, stirring everything around.

Add your ginger and then put your garlic. Allow this to fry for 2 minutes or so, stirring to make sure that it doesn't stick.

Now add the turmeric, cumin and curry powder and mix this together. It will likely start to stick at this point so add 1/2 glass of water at this point. Cover the pot, let it cook for 5 minutes on the medium heat, check to make sure that everything is bubbling away nicely, then reduce the heat to low. Cook covered for 1/2 hour.

After 1/2 hour, stir everything again. Your octopus pieces will now swim in deep brown, very aromatic sauce.

Add 1 teaspoonful of salt to the mixture and also add the tin of chopped tomatoes. Stir this well and allow this to cook gently over a low flame for another 1/2 hour. Make sure you put the lid back on.

After this time stir the finished octopus curry once more, admiring the gorgeous aroma and rich deep colour, sprinkle with the chopped coriander remove from heat and allow to stand for a few minutes.

You can eat this special dish with plain boiled rice and a vegetable of some sort. A bowl of light bouillon is a very good accompaniment.

Octopus Cooked in the Pickling Style

When I finished studying for my acupuncture qualification I went to Mauritius with Rachel and Michael - friends that I had made on the course. One day my cousin Din (Pronounced Gin) took us out for a picnic and we drove around the island going from beauty spot to beauty spot eating and drinking along the way. One of the very tasty dishes that he had prepared for us was this Octopus cCooked in the Pickling Style. Here is that recipe, fresh, marine and succulent.

Best eaten from a paper plate *au bord de la mer.*

Ingredients:

- 1 large octopus, cleaned with the head off
- 2 cups of water
- 1 cinnamon stick
- 1 onion
- Sprinkle of salt
- Juice of 1 lemon, or 1 lemon sliced finely
- ½ bunch of coriander, finely chopped
- 3 tomatoes, finely chopped
- 1-2 green chillis, finely chopped

This dish will serve 4 day trippers as part of a buffet of picnic delights.

Method:

In a pressure cooker, bring your water to boil. Do not add any salt to this otherwise your dish will be far too salty. Add the stick of cinnamon. When it is boiling add the octopus. Close the lid and allow this to cook on medium for 15 -20 minutes or so until the steam comes out 2 times at least. Check to make sure that your octopus is nice and tender. If its still a bit tough, cover and boil again for another 3-5 minutes.

Now, make your vinaigrette.

In a cup mix together your lemon juice (or finely chopped lemon), sprinkle of salt, your coriander, tomato and chillis. Mix this well.

When just about to serve (or about to set out on your day trip or your picnic) toss the octopus in the vinaigrette and mix everything together. Fresh, succulent and flavoursome. Eat this with some crusty bread to mop up the tangy sauce and a super cold Phoenix beer.

Din's Recipe for Octopus Curry

My cousin Din worked for the Ministry of Fish and would guard the coral reefs from the scourge of illegal fishing. He whips up the freshest and most delicious fish curries, frying the fish outside in his back yard, his trusty wok emanating delicious smells and sizzles.

This recipe will serve 4 people. Serve it with rice, bread and some plain cooked vegetables. It is slightly saucier than my mum's version and is less rich. Curry powder is not used to make this - the curry flavour comes from the curry leaves.

Ingredients:

- 2 onions
- 1 inch of ginger, peeled and grated finely
- 4 cloves of garlic, crushed and finely chopped
- 2 teaspoonful of cumin seeds
- 4 - 5 tomatoes, chopped
- Water
- Salt
- Small bunch of curry leaves
- 1 chilli, sliced lengthways
- 3 tablespoonfuls of vegetable oil

Method:

This meal requires the use of a pressure cooker. It will take far too long to prepare without one. If you don't have one, you really do need to buy one.

In a pressure cooker, bring your water to boil. My mum cautions you to not add any salt to this otherwise your dish will be far too salty. Add the stick of cinnamon. When the water comes to the boil add the octopus. Close the lid, making sure that you attach the little weight to the top, and allow this to cook on a medium heat for 15 - 20 minutes or so - the steam needs to come wooshing out at least twice. Remove from the heat and when it's safe to do so check to make sure that the octopus has cooked sufficiently - the tough tentacles need to become nice and tender. If it's still a bit rubbery no need to worry- simply cover and boil again for a minute or so. When it is done drain away the water and set the octopus aside.

Now, it is time to prepare your rougaille… (that's what Mauritians call a curry sauce). Dry fry your cumin seeds over a medium heat until they have turned a lovely deep brown colour and have released their wonderful warming aroma. Set them aside when they are done.

Add the oil to the frying pan and heat over a medium flame. Fry the onions in this for 5 minutes, stirring occasionally until they have turned a golden brown colour. Don't allow them to burn or go crisp. Now, add the garlic, ginger and cumin and allow this to fry together whilst mixing it all together. After a minute or so, when it feels like everything is starting to stick to the pan add the chopped tomatoes and the curry leaves.

Now add 1/4 cup of water to your octopus, taste everything and sprinkle in some salt to taste - a tiny bit at a time as it won't need very much. Bring everything to the boil once more, reduce the heat to a low flame, cover and allow to simmer for a final 10 minutes at which point it will be beautifully cooked.

DELICIOUS MAURITIUS

Just before it's time to sit down and eat, sprinkle with the chopped coriander.

Rice

From elaborate vegetable biriyanis that take hours to prepare, to sizzling fried rice that is wok fried in moments, there are a number of scrumptious rice dishes that are particularly Mauritian in feeling and flavour.

- Kitcheri
- Chicken Biriyani
- Vegetable Biriyani
- Lamb Biriyani
- Fish Biriyani
- Mauritian Fried Rice
- Vinaigrette Sauce for Fried Rice
- Noodles with Chicken and Prawns
- Easy Peasy Rice with Cumin and Cardamon
- Chicken Risotto

Kitcheri

Pronounced Kitch-che-ree

Kitcheri is a bright yellow rice dish, simple to make and economical to boot. It is soft and easily digested which makes it just right for one of those lazy days or if you are person with a delicate constitution. My mum warns that this meal needs to be eaten as soon as it is cooked otherwise it will set into a pudding consistency. Eat it as it is or perhaps with a spoonful of coconut chutney. A nice egg daube also goes well.

This recipe will serve 2 people. It is easy to scale it up if you want to make it for more people.

Ingredients:

- 1/2 cup of white basmati rice
- 1/2 cup of split red lentils
- 1 teaspoonful of turmeric powder
- 1 medium onion, finely chopped
- 1/2 teaspoonful of salt
- 2 tablespoonful of vegetable oil
- 2 cups of water

Method:

Wash the rice and the lentils together thoroughly. Swirl them around in a few changes of water and then drain the water away carefully.

Warm the oil in a small frying pan and add the onion to this. Fry it until it is golden, don't let it get too dark. When the onion is cooked switch the heat off.

Now add 2 cups of water to the rice mixture, sprinkle in the turmeric and the salt to your rice and lentil mixture and bring this to a boil over a medium flame. When it starts to boil lower the heat and cook this uncovered for 10 minutes. Towards the end of the cooking time, stir this regularly as kitcheri is prone to sticking.

Add the onion together with its cooking oil to the rice and lentil mixture and stir this around. The kitcheri needs to have a soft consistency, the rice and lentils need to take on a thick soupy consistency. Think of a very soft risotto and you will be almost there. If it has gone too dry, no need to fret - simply add a spash more water.

Chicken Biriyani

Chicken Bree-yaa-nee

Biriyani (or biri to its friends) is a fancy, highly spiced chicken and rice dish. To make this dish properly does require takes effort - mountains of herbs and vegetables have to be prepared and it needs to be lovingly tended whilst it steams to perfection, but the results are certainly worthwhile. The resulting long grained rice is glamorous and moist, studded with whole spices and streaked with saffron, the chicken is perfectly succulent and the fragrance divine.

My mum uses a massive pan known as a dekchi to cook this. It is the size of two large pressure cookers put together and is perfect for feeding her brood - in total there are 13 of us in my family. Her dekchi has a heavy bottom and is so large that it lives in the cellar and hauled out by my dad when a birthday or a similar excuse for a party approaches. If you are cooking for a smaller number of people you won't need to use such a colossal vessel. Simply use your largest and heaviest pan.

This recipe will serve 4 people

Ingredients:

- 8 pieces of skinless chicken legs or thighs (these are the most moist bits)
- 5 medium onions, sliced finely
- 1/2 cup of frozen peas
- 3 medium potatoes peeled and cut in halves
- 7-8 cloves of garlic, crushed and chopped

- A big cube of ginger, 1 inches long. Scraped and grated roughly
- 3 tablespoonfuls of cumin seeds
- 1 teaspoonful of chilli powder (leave this out if you don't like it too hot)
- 6 cloves
- 6 whole cardamon pods - crushed to release the juice
- 1 1/2 sticks of cinnamon
- 2 tablespoonfuls of yoghurt
- 1/4 bunch - roughly 10 sprigs of coriander chopped finely. My mum says that if it's a small bunch, put in 1/2 a bunch.
- 10 sprigs of fresh mint roughly 2 inches long each
- 2 teaspoonful of salt
- 2 cups of basmati rice, not brown rice, white basmati rice (500g)
- 1 cup of oil (300ml)
- 1/4 packet of butter. Some people prefer to use use ghee - personally I can't bear the taste
- 2 pinches of saffron

Method:

Wash the rice thoroughly and then soak it for at least 1/2 an hour before you start to cook. This will enable your biri to cook quicker.

The first secret to a great biri is fried onions. We are going to fry them in two batches - if you add them all in one go they won't go crispy enough. So you need to take your time about it. Heat the cup of oil in a frying pan over a medium flame. When the oil starts to smoke slightly add half of your finely chopped onions. You need to fry them for between 5 - 10 minutes, stirring occasionally. The onions will go crispy and turn a deep golden brown colour. Once your first batch of onions have reached the desired colour and texture remove them for the oil using a slotted spoon and set them

DELICIOUS MAURITIUS

aside on a dry plate. Repeat this process this with the second batch of onions.

Pour the oniony oil out of the frying pan and reserve this in a cup - this oil will be used at a later point. You don't need to wash out the pan out. Add the chicken to this frying pan and sprinkle with salt. Turn the heat to medium and gently warm the chicken until the fats (that's the way my mum says it!) have come out of the chicken. This will take between 10 - 15minutes and you need to turn the chicken pieces over mid way. Remove the chicken from the frying pan and set aside.

Prick the potatoes using a fork or sharp knife and add them to the same frying pan. If there is any oil left in the pan from frying the chicken that's great - if it is all looking a bit dry add a little more oil. Gently fry the potatoes for about 5 minutes turning them over from time to time. Remove from the pan and pop on top of the warmed chicken pieces.

Pull out the biggest pot that you own. As everything is now going to be cooked in one pot is does need to be pretty big - 10 inches high x 12 inches across is a good starting point. This is your dekchi. Pre heat this pan over a low flame for a couple of minutes.

Into your warmed dekchi, pour in the reserved cooking oil. Allow this to heat up until it starts to smoke slightly. Toss in almost all of your cumin seeds (make sure that you save 1 teaspoonful) and allow these seeds to sizzle in the hot oil - just one minute is enough. They will release a lovely aroma and frying them will intensify the flavour of the cumin.

Add the ginger, garlic, yoghurt, 1/2 of the fried onions, 1 stick of the cinnamon, 4 cardamon seeds, 4 cloves, and mix this in with the sizzling cumin seeds.

Now add your warmed chicken and potatoes to the dekchi, add the peas and mix everything around well making sure that the chicken is well coated.

Pour over enough water to cover the chicken mixture and stir this around. It will prevent everything sticking and burning. Now add the salt, chilli powder and the chopped coriander and mint. Stir this all together, remove from the heat and put to one side.

Now it is time for us to prepare the rice. In a new pan we bring to the boil 1 1/2 pints of water. Add a teaspoonful of salt, the remaining 1/2 stick of cinnamon, 2 cardamons, 2 cloves and teaspoonful of cumin. Allow this to boil away merrily on high heat.

Using a sieve, drain the water away from rice that you have previously washed and soaked. Add this rice to the bubbling spicy water and bring it back to the boil. Let it continue boiling on high for a further 5 minutes.

Remove the rice from the heat and using your trusty sieve, drain away the excess water. Don't worry - the rice is not meant to be fully cooked at this point.

We now return to your chicken and spice filled dekchi. Layer the par-cooked rice gently over the chicken mixture. Don't pat it down, just gently spoon the rice over. What you are aiming for is a separate layer of rice that will then steam over the cooking chicken mixture.

Make a hole in the middle of the rice and pour 2 cups of water into this hole. Cover the dekchi, turn up the heat to high and bring to the boil and then continue boiling away for a further 5 minutes. Now sprinkle the saffron on top of the cooking rice and lower the heat to medium.

Cook for on medium for 10 minutes. Split the knob of butter into 4 bits and lay this on top of the rice evenly. Lower the heat to low and cook for a further 1/2 hour.

DELICIOUS MAURITIUS

Check to see if the rice has cooked, if it has, then the biriyani has cooked. If the rice hasn't cooked yet, stir the top of the rice gently (not mixing up the chicken) and cook for a few minutes more. Once the rice has cooked sprinkle the remaining fried onions over the top. (If you want to be fancy, you can sprinkle the remaining onions on each plate as a fancy garnish) And put the put the lid back on until you are ready to serve.

This now brings us to the second secret to great biri: It is all in the serving: Never just serve from the top. If you do this, then that poor person will just get a serving of rice. You need to start digging in from the bottom of the pan. Alternatively you can pile everything out onto a serving plate and mix it up gently to ensure that everyone gets a bit of everything.

Vegetable Biriyani

Vegetable Bree-yaa-nee

Many Mauritian people serve this special vegetarian rice dish on religious days of the year as you don't eat meat on those sorts of days. A typical Mauritian wedding will last three days and on the first day neither meat nor alcohol are served - There is plenty of time for boozing on the ensuing days.

When my sister Prema and her fiancé Neil got married my mum prepared this for the evening party which was held in a tiny marquee in the back garden of her new home. The night before the wedding I helped my mum and dad to quietly prepare the mountain of vegetables that were needed. Topping and tailing and talking quietly.

Eat this with some coconut chutney or just on its own. If you have it for breakfast the next morning then you can serve it with a runny fried egg on top - oh that is so tasty. Think of it as a Mauritian version of kedgeree.

This recipe will serve 4 - 6 people

Ingredients:

- 1 lb of French beans, topped and tailed, and sliced lengthways (or if this is beyond your cutting skills you can chop then into 1/2 inch pieces) The lengthways cut does look more elegant though
- 1/2 cabbage, finely shredded. A green cabbage tastes nicer but at a push a white one will work fine
- 2 medium carrots cut into juliennes

- 3 medium potatoes, peeled and cut into quarters
- 1/2 cup of peas
- 5 medium onions, sliced finely
- 7-8 cloves of garlic, crushed and chopped
- A big cube of ginger, 1 inches long. Scraped and grated roughly
- 3 tablespoonfuls of cumin seeds
- 1 teaspoonful of chilli powder (you can leave this out if you don't like your food too hot)
- 8 cloves
- 8 whole cardamon crushed to release the juice
- 1 1/2 sticks of cinnamon
- 2 tablespoonfuls of yoghurt
- 1/4 bunch - or roughly 10 sprigs - of fresh coriander, finely chopped
- 10 sprigs of fresh mint roughly 2 inches long each
- 2 teaspoonful of salt
- 2 cups (roughly 500g) of white basmati rice, not brown rice
- 1 cup of oil (300ml)
- 1/4 packet of butter
- 2 pinches of saffron

Method:

Soak your rice in water for at least 1/2 hour before you start.

Add 2 tablespoonfuls of oil to a large frying pan and heat over a medium flame. When the oil is hot, add the chopped potatoes. Prick the potatoes deeply using a fork or sharp knife, and fry these, stirring occasionally for 5 minutes. They may turn a pale golden colour. Remove the potatoes from the oil and allow to drain.

Add the drained potatoes to a big cooking pot and add the following:

All of the cabbage, beans, carrots, garlic, ginger, chilli powder, yoghurt, coriander and mint. Mix this together well and then sprinkle on most of the cumin, setting aside 1 teaspoonful to use later on.

Now add 6 of your cloves, 6 cardamon pods and 1 stick of cinnamon.

Heat all of the remaining oil in your frying pan under a medium flame until it is hot. When it smokes slightly add half of the sliced onions. Fry these, stirring occasionally to make sure that they don't stick and burn, for around 5 minutes until they have turned a deep golden brown. Don't let them get too crispy, you are searching for succulence not going for the burn.

Now remove these onions from the frying pan using a slotted spoon and sprinkle this evenly all over the vegetables in your cooking pot.

Now fry the remaining onions in the same way. Once they are cooked remove from the oil and set aside. Don't throw the remaining oil away.

Now it's onto the rice. Put the kettle on and boil 1 litre of water.

Use a sieve to drain away all of the water from the soaking rice.

Once the kettle has come to the boil pour the boiling water into a pan and add the salt, the remaining 2 cloves, 2 cardamons and the remaining 1/2 cinnamon stick. Bring it all back to the boil on a high heat and then add the rice. When it returns to to boil again and starts to bubble quickly quickly, remove from the heat and using your trusty sieve drain away the boiling water. This will take around 1 - 2 minutes.

Now gently spoon the rice over the vegetables. Don't press or pat anything down.

Sprinkle the saffron into a cup of boiling water and allow to soak for a minute. Pour this saffron infused water over your rice.

DELICIOUS MAURITIUS

Pour the remaining oil around the circumference of the pan and make a couple of holes in the rice/ vegetable mixture and pour oil into the holes. This will help to ensure that the biriyani does not stick and well as enriching the finished dish.

Cut the butter into 10 cubes and dot this over the rice.

We are almost there.

Carefully return your cooking pot to the hob, cover and turn on the heat to a medium flame. Allow to cook for 10 minutes - or until steam starts to be released. At this point lower the heat to a low flame and cook for 1/2 an hour slowly slowly. Look at it and see if the rice has cooked, if it has not, then allow to cook for another 15 minutes.

Et…Volia! Your Vegetable Biriyani will be cooked. Your rice will be perfectly steamed, glistening yellow and spicy. Make sure that you serve your Biriyani from the bottom of the pan up - if you just serve from the top some poor person will just get a plate of rice which isn't very hospitable: Make sure you scoop properly and dig deep to release the plethora of vegetables you spent so long preparing.

Serve with a splash of chutney, a simple mint or coconut chutney goes well. Tuck in and devour with relish.

Lamb Biriyani

Lamb Bree-yaa-nee

This is a very simple way of preparing Biriyani. You wouldn't guess it from the taste which is just as succulent as the more elaborate ways that you can cook it.

This recipe will serve 4-5 people

- 1½ lb of lamb chopped into inch size cubes
- 5 medium onions, finely sliced (not diced)
- ½ cup of frozen peas
- 4 - 5 smallish potatoes peeled and cut in halves
- 7-8 cloves of garlic, crushed and chopped
- A big cube of ginger, 1 inch long. Scraped and grated roughly
- 3 tablespoonfuls of cumin seeds
- 1 teaspoonful of chilli powder (you can leave this out if you don't like your food too hot)
- 6 cloves
- 6 whole cardamon crushed to release the seeds - my mum does this by nibbling them a little
- 1½ sticks of cinnamon
- 2 tablespoonfuls of yoghurt
- 1/4 bunch - roughly 10 sprigs of coriander chopped finely
- 10 sprigs of fresh mint roughly 2 inches long each
- 2 teaspoonfuls of salt plus 1 to boil the rice in
- 2 cups of basmati rice, not brown rice, white basmati rice 500g

DELICIOUS MAURITIUS

- 1 1/2 cups of oil (300ml)
- 1/4 packet of butter. If you like, you can substitute this with ghee.
- 2 pinches of saffron
- 2 chillis, sliced lengthways

Method:

Put your rice to soak in a pan of water. It needs to soak for at least an hour before cooking

Pour 1 cup of oil into a deep frying pan and heat under a medium flame. When the oil heats up add all of the onions. Fry them, stirring occasionally until they have softened and are a nice medium brown colour. Don't let them go too crispy. Remove the onions from the oil and set aside.

Prick the potatoes all over using a knife or a fork. Make sure that you go in quite deeply. This will help them to cook quicker. Put these aside.

Now, put the kettle on. Boil the water. Pour this into a pan and add 1 teaspoonful of salt, 1 teaspoonful of your cumin seeds, 2 cloves, 2 cardamons, and 1/2 a cinnamon stick. Drain your soaked rice using a sieve and then add this rice to the pan of spicy water. Bring this to the boil again over a high flame and as soon as it starts to boil take it off the heat and drain it again into your sieve. Set this rice aside.

Take out your heavy bottom pan. Add 1/2 cup of oil. Heat this up. When it is hot add your Lamb and potatoes together with 1 tablespoonful of your cooked onion. Allow to sizzle gently together for 5 minutes over a medium flame stirring this around occasionally.

Next, stirring all the while add your garlic, ginger, cumin, then all the rest of the spices Now add the yoghurt, chilli powder, chillis, coriander and mint. Stir. Add 2 cups of cold water to the pan now and bring everything to boil over a high flame. When it starts to bubble vigorously spoon your rice over the top. Don't stir this in as the rice needs to cook in its very own layer. Using the handle of a spoon poke a couple of holes in the rice reaching all the way down to the bottom. This will enable steam to rise and for your biriani to cook throughly.

Quickly, sprinkle over the remaining onions and drizzle any remaining oil around the sides and over the top as evenly as you can. Add the peas in a thin layer over the top, sprinkle your saffron over everything, and finally chop up your butter into about 10 cubes and dot these around evenly over the surface. Cover your pan with its lid. Biriyani cooks in its steam so don't forget this step!

Lower the heat now to medium and allow to cook until you see some steam escaping from the lid. Now lower the heat again to its lowest possible setting and allow everything to cook in its own steam for about 15 - 20 minutes or until your rice is done.

DELICIOUS MAURITIUS

Fish Biriyani

There is a variation on biriyani made with fish, but my mum doesn't know much about it. We imagine that you will need to fry the fish thoroughly first and then cook in the same way as the Lamb Biriyani. I don't like fish biriyani with the skin on or any bones, so I would remove these. The fish would need to be sliced and you would use a fish like red snapper or tuna. King prawns might also work.

Mauritian Fried Rice

Your kitchen will be a hot, steamy mess after making this dish as there is so much chopping, and preparing of different components to do. But it is worth it as Mauritian style fried rice is Glorious. Plump prawns, moist marinaded chicken and slivers of fried egg…It is my favourite thing to eat in the world and I can shovel down mountains (should that be Long Mountains?) of the stuff!

This is not my mum's recipe. This is my mum's cousin's recipe. This cousin is called Amrita and she runs a local snack bar. When my mum goes to visit she will stand in Amrita's kitchen and chat to her whilst she cooks. Customers think that my mum works there. She doesn't. She's just gossiping.

This recipe will serve 4 big eaters.

Ingredients:

All of the ingredients in this recipe are finely chopped because the key to getting a perfect fried rice is to cook everything over a high heat and to do so very quickly. My mum recited this recipe at such high speed that my typing couldn't keep up. By speaking so fast she was demonstrating the speed of preparing this dish. So remember: Quick quick.

For the fried rice:

- 2 cups of white basmati rice, washed
- 2 onions, finely chopped
- 1 bunch of spring onion, finely chopped
- 1 pepper, chopped into small pieces (the size of a pea)

DELICIOUS MAURITIUS

145

- 5 mushrooms, finely sliced
- 3 cloves of garlic crushed and finely chopped
- 2 tablespoonful of Soy sauce
- 2 tablespoonful of oyster sauce
- 1 teaspoonful of salt
- 1/2 lb of chicken diced into 1/2 inch cubes.
- 10 big juicy king prawns (raw or cooked)
- 3 eggs
- 4-5 tablespoonful of vegetable oil
- A small glass of water

Note: You will need to use a big wok

Method:

First cook your rice. Add 4 cups of water to your pan and add your rice. Bring this to the boil over a high heat. Once it has started to boil reduce the heat to low. Cook it uncovered for around 10 minutes. If after this time it hasn't cooked, let it simmer again for another 5 minutes. Remove the rice from the heat, drain it, and leave the rice to cool down completely in a colander.

Now, crack your eggs in a bowl, whisk them round with a fork, sprinkle with some salt and fry this in your wok turning it over occasionally until it is a well cooked omelette. Set this omelette aside and let it cool.

It is now time for you to start cooking. The preparation takes most of the time. Cooking it all up only takes a few minutes. Now, if there are spelling mistakes in this recipe blame my mum - she was dictating this recipe at double fast speed to demonstrate how quick quick this meal needs to be made…

Add the rest of the oil to the wok and turn the heat to high. Let the oil heat up and start to smoke and sizzle. First add your onions and fry these, stirring regularly for 1 minute.

Now, add your chicken to the wok and stir this around mixing everything thoroughly. You are stirring everything quickly quickly as the heat is high and you don't want everything to stick. Cook this for another minute. Now add the prawns and cook for another minute quick quick. If you use raw prawns they will turn a gorgeous rosey pink as they become ready.

Now add the mushrooms, pepper, garlic, salt, soya and oyster sauce and stir this well for a minute. Stir it quickly quickly. It it starts to burn or sizzle too much sprinkle over a few spoonfuls of water to calm things down.

Now add the cooled rice. Stir this all together quickly and cook for 2 minutes. The rice will heat up from both the wok and also the residual heat of the rest of the ingredients. Once you are happy that everything is piping hot your work here is done. Remove the wok from the heat, dab the sweat from your brow and dish out your fried rice, piling everything in to 4 warmed plates.

Cut up the omelette into quarters and then tear these into smaller pieces and decorate each mountain of fried rice with this.

Finally, garnish with your spring onions, sprinkle with some teaspoonful of your vinaigrette (the recipe for this is below) and enjoy the true taste of Mauritius on a plate.

DELICIOUS MAURITIUS

Vinaigrette Sauce for Fried Rice

This simple sauce adds perfect piquancy to fried rice. Sprinkle it over liberally and tuck in.

This will be enough for 4 people.

Ingredients:

- 1 tablespoonful of vinegar
- 4 cloves of garlics, finely chopped
- 4 chillis, finely chopped - it needs to be hot
- 1/2 teaspoonful of salt
- 4 tablespoonfuls of water

Method:

Mix everything together!

Serve in a little bowl with a baby spoon and sprinkle liberally over your fried rice.

Noodles with Chicken and Prawns

You might be a little surprised to find noodles in a chapter about rice. I however view these noodles as a Close Cousin to Fried Rice which is why they are here. This is a very tasty dish and a very easy way to eat up a pile of greens, hidden amongst the glistening noodles. All the different coloured vegetables are very pretty and make this a very healthy and extremely filling meal. This is particularly good with a few squirts of hot chilli sauce - or a splash of home made chilli vinaigrette.

This recipe will sate 2 hungry appetites. Scale up if you need to cook for more people. Just be aware that you want to make this for a lot of people that you will need to have a gigantic wok to fry it all in, or be prepared to dish up and serve people at different times.

Ingredients:

- 1/2 packet of egg noodles
- 1/2 onion, chopped finely
- 2 cloves of garlic, crushed and finely chopped
- 1 medium carrot, peeled and cut into slim batons
- 1/8th of a green cabbage - shredded
- 2 mushrooms, sliced
- 1/2 red pepper, sliced thinly (Use a red pepper as it will look prettier)
- 2 tablespoonfuls of soy sauce - add more to taste if necessary

DELICIOUS MAURITIUS

- 2 spring onions, chopped finely
- 2 eggs, beaten
- 1 chicken breast, skinned boned and thinly chopped, as thin as you can cut it
- 4 huge tiger prawns - deveined and detrained, or 8 normal sized king prawns
- A small handful of beansprouts
- 4 tablespoonful of vegetable oil

Method:

First of all put a pan of water to boil. When it is boiling stick in your noodles and cook them according to the instructions. When they are cooked, drain and set aside.

Now, you fry your egg. Heat up the vegetable oil in your wok and fry up your beaten eggs. When they are beautifully fried and a golden yellow colour remove then from the oil, and cut them lengthwise into slices 2cm thick. Set them aside.

Add the onions to the wok, and fry them over a high flame. Stir this around for 30 seconds. Now add the chicken and prawns. Cook this for 2-3 minutes, stirring continuously.

Now, add the cabbage, carrot, garlic, pepper, mushroom and beansprouts. Stir this over a high heat for 5 minutes. Add the soy sauce now. If it looks as if it is going to burn or stick, add a splash of water. Keep stirring.

Now, mix in the cooked noodles and stir this around well. Everything will be sizzling and cooking away merrily. Keep cooking this over a high heat for 2 - 3 minutes until the noodles are hot. Just before serving add the egg and fry this together for 1 minute more.

Serve your noodles now, sprinkling them with your chopped spring onion.

If you want to make this for a particularly special meal, serve it with some freshly fried prawn crackers and sprinkle your noodles with some chilli sauce to make everything zing.

Dinner is served. If you have a gong, now would be a suitable time to bang it.

Easy Peasy Rice with Cumin and Cardamon

Sometimes the most simple things are the most marvellous. Like going for a paddle in the sea, or plucking and eating a fruit that's still warm from the sun…Or being able to cook rice perfectly. If you find it impossible to cook rice then this recipe is for you.

No rice cooker and absolutely no fuss. If you follow this simple recipe you too will be able to produce mountains of perfectly fluffed rice every. single. time.

This recipe will serve 4 people and is the perfect foil for your spicy curry and any other saucy dish of your choosing.

Ingredients:

- 1 cup of basmati rice, rinsed in several changes of water
- 2 cups of water
- Couple of pinches of salt
- 2 tablespoonful of vegetable oil

Optional extras:

- 1 tablespoonful of cumin seeds
- 2 cardamon pods, nibbled open, as my mother does, to release the aroma

Method:

Add the oil to your pan and heat this up over a high flame. When the oil is hot, add the cumin and cardamon. Stir these around for about 1 minute using your wooden spoon. There will be a beautiful warmly spiced aroma. Don't allow the seeds to burn!

Next add the rinsed rice and stir everything around for one minute more. You may notice that the rice grains may start to stick a bit. Don't worry, we will sort this out in a moment.

Now add the water, salt, and stir everything again making sure that you use your wooden spoon to release any stuck grains of rice from their watery grave at the bottom of the pan.

We will now bring our mixture to the boil uncovered. As soon as it starts to bubble vigorously turn the heat down to the lowest possible heat setting, cover up and allow to simmer for 20 minutes.

After 20 minutes, take a peep at Sleeping Beauty - rice so white, fluffy and light, peppered with ebony specks of cumin. I use a fork to serve it - the rice grains seem to stay more separate that way.

Serve immediately.

Chicken Risotto

Pronounced Chicken Riz-otto

This recipe was given to my mum in 1967 by an Italian friend and it has been in our family ever since then. Alongside the recipe, this Italian friend gave my mum the gift of a handful of green beans that she had just plucked from her garden. My mum cooked those beans that same day in this risotto - the first time that she had ever made it. To this day she remembers fondly the tenderness of those green beans.

This recipe will serve 4 people

Ingredients:

- 1 lb of basmati rice (not risotto rice)
- 1 tablespoonful of mixed herbs
- 1 chicken stock cube
- 3 cups of water
- 2 medium carrots, peeled and diced
- 1/2 lb of green beans, topped and tailed and chopped into 1 inch lengths
- 1/2 lb mushrooms, sliced
- 1/2 can of tomatoes
- 2 onions, diced
- 4 chicken legs and thighs, skinned with the bone in
- 4 king prawns in their shell
- 1 tablespoonful of salt
- 3 tablespoonfuls of oil

Method:

First warm your chicken and prawns in a frying pan over a low flame for 5 minutes turning occasionally. Drain away any fat that is released. Remove from the heat.

Add the oil to a large heavy bottomed pan and heat on a medium flame for a minute or so until the oil is hot. Add the onion and stir this around for a couple of minutes and allow them to soften slightly.

Now add the chicken and allow to cook for 5 minutes turning occasionally.

Sprinkle over the mixed herbs and the stock cube now, add the tomatoes and stir this and allow to cook for another 5 minutes. Now add the water and bring this to the boil. Let it boil away for 5 further minutes.

Add all of the vegetables to the pot now and stir everything well. Once more bring to the boil - you can wash and drain rice in a few changes of water whilst you wait.

When the vegetables reach boiling point add the rice. Put the lid on and allow it to…yes, you've guessed it, reach boiling point.

As soon as you see steam coming from the pan and everything starts to bubble away (this will take about 15 minutes) turn the heat very low, cover again and let it simmer for a final 15 minutes.

Eat with a squirt of ketchup or some chilli sauce. *Delicioso.*

Cakes and Sweets

The sugar cane plant was introduced to Mauritius by the Dutch in 1939 and Mauritians have not looked back since! Huge swathes of the island are covered with sugar cane plantations and many members of my family have tended to these fields over the years.

Mauritians adore sugary treats and puddings so it is no wonder that my mum is a bit of an expert confectioner. Although Mauritius is a religiously diverse country most of its population are Hindu like my family. During Hindu religious ceremonies vast quantities of these treats are made to be presented as offerings - to be gobbled up after the event by the faithful congregation.

These recipes are suitable for pious and non pious people alike - and all of them taste divine.

- Manbogh
- Khaja
- Banana Loaf Cake
- Gulab Jamun
- Jilabi
- Besan Ladoo
- Gateau Batat
- Kheer
- Tukmaria
- Poa
- Tekwa
- Tekwa Dal
- Corn Pudding

- Napolitaines
- Satwa
- Semolina balls

Manbogh

Pronounced Mun-bow-gh

Manbogh is a soft and cuddly sort of dessert studded with an occasional nut and sultana treasure. As this is a very filling pudding it is perfect to feed hungry hordes at tea time. Simple to make you can whip this up in less than 10 minutes. My youngest sister Benny is particularly fond of Manbogh.

This recipe will fill the bellies of four ravenous beasts.

Ingredients:

- 1 cup of plain white flour
- 1/2 cup of ground almonds
- 1/4 cup of sultanas
- 1/4 cup of roughly chopped almonds with the skins on
- 1/4 cup of roughly chopped raw cashew nuts
- 1/4 teaspoonful of elychee powder - this is the Mauritian name for Cardamon
- 4 tablespoonfuls of butter
- 1/4 cup of sugar
- 1 cup of whole milk
- 1/2 cup of water
- 2 cloves

Method:

First you need to toast your flour. Do this by heating your pan over a fairly low flame: if your pan is too hot it can lead to scorching.

When the pan has warmed up add the flour and stir this around until it turns a medium golden brown colour. You will notice that the smell intensifies and becomes rather lovely…so much so that when my mum was little she would eat the toasted flour as it was. (My sister Benny and I went one better on the oddness scale and when we were little we would secretly eat spoonfuls of *non-* toasted flour!)

Once your flour has reached the desired shade remove from the hot pan and sieve it into a bowl. If you keep the flour in the pan it will carry on browning and will possibly burn.

Next add 2 tablespoonfuls of butter to your clean pan. Heat this over a medium flame. When the butter has melted slightly add the chopped almonds and cashew nuts. Allow this to cook for a minute, stirring it around.

Then add the sultanas and stir for another minute.

Let us now add the milk, water, sugar, cloves and elychee powder and bring this to a boil on a medium flame stirring occasionally and cook like this for 2-3 minutes.

Now all at once add your toasted flour to the boiling mixture and stir everything consistently until all of the liquid has been absorbed. Keep on stirring until your mixture reaches a soft consistency and there is no more separate liquid in the pan. Finally add the remaining butter, give a last few stirs and its done.

Serve a large tablespoonful of this to everyone and they will be happy.

DELICIOUS MAURITIUS

Khaja

Pronounced Kha-jah

Khaja are sweet crunchy snacks that children absolutely love to eat. They are made in inordinate quantities at Divali or other religious ceremonies when you might invite over a gaggle of friends and family. When my mum was little so many people would come to visit that her neighbours would come over to help with the rolling out.

This recipe will make 12 Khaja.

Ingredients:

- ½ lb of plain flour, sieved (1 large mug)
- 2 tablespoonfuls of vegetable oil or melted butter
- 1 pinch of bicarbonate of soda
- 8-9 tablespoonfuls of water
- A couple of spoonfuls of oil to brush with
- 2 cups of vegetable oil for frying

For the syrup:

- ½ lb of sugar (1 small cup)
- 2 cups of water
- 2 slightly crushed cardamon pods

Method:

First make your syrup.

Bring the water, sugar and cardamon to boil in a pan over a high flame. Stir it occasionally. When it starts to boil reduce the heat to low. As you stir you will notice the syrup changing consistency and colour. It will start to darken and become slightly thicker and stickier in consistency. When it reaches this point remove from the heat. Allow to cool and set aside.

Mix the flour, oil and bicarb together in a mixing bowl. Use your fingers and create breadcrumbs.

Add the water little by little and keep mixing it together with your fingers until you have a medium-firm dough. Don't add all of the water at once - you might not need it all. Cover and set this dough aside - don't refrigerate it - and leave it to rest for 15-20 minutes.

Once the dough has had its beauty sleep split it into two parts. Roll each part out into a rectangular shape roughly the size of a sheet of A4 paper. Once you have reached this size brush the top with the vegetable oil or melted butter.

Holding the dough horizontally, start rolling it into itself. We are not talking about using a rolling pin here - think of rolling Cleopatra in her rug. Start off with an initial 1/2 inch fold and keep going from there until you have created a long horizontal tube shape.

Cut this tube into 6 equal pieces. If you like you can trim the edges so that everything looks equal, but it isn't necessary.

Sprinkle your board and rolling pin with more flour. Take one of your slices and place so that you can't see any of the cut sides - you don't want to see a swirl, you want to see the flat side. Roll this out very gently and without squashing it any more than necessary, until it lengthens to about 3 inches long. You don't want it to get any wider if possible.

DELICIOUS MAURITIUS

Repeat until you have rolled out all of the dough in this way. You are now ready to fry.

In a wok heat the oil over a medium flame. The oil should not smoke. When it has reached the correct heat add the Khaja using your fingers to slowly slide them into the hot oil. Add 2 - 3 at a time, more if you have a large wok. The Khaja will sink to the bottom and start to bubble away. In about 2 minutes they will rise to the top of the oil. This is a sign that they are ready to turn over. Turn using a fish slice and allow to fry for another 2- 3 minutes and turn ever minute or so. When ready they will turn a golden brown colour. Do not allow them to go any darker than this.

Remove using a slotted spoon, drain off excess oil and transfer to a wire rack.

When you have finished frying all of your Khaja, dip them briefly into the cooled syrup -1 second is enough -and make sure that all of the surfaces are well coated. Remove from the syrup, and arrange on your party plate.

Khaja can last for a couple of weeks if stored in an airtight container.

Banana Loaf Cake

Moist, sweet and delightfully rich, this banana cake is perfect to eat with a cup of fine Mauritian tea. If you have a bunch of bananas that are far too ripe, then now is the perfect time to make this cake. This recipe will make 8 fine slices. My mum has reduced the amount of sugar and butter in this recipe - and it still tastes marvellous.

Ingredients:

- 70g of soft unsalted butter (salted will work at a pinch)
- 100g of caster sugar
- 2 eggs, beaten
- 250g of plain flour, sieved
- 1 tablespoonful of baking powder
- ½ teaspoonful of bicarbonate of sofa
- 3 ripe bananas, mashed
- ½ teaspoonful of vanilla essence
- Zest of one orange and one lemon, grated finely
- 2oz of chopped walnuts - roughly chopped or broken please

Method:

Preheat the oven to 350.

Mix the butter and sugar together until they are a lovely creamy texture. Slowly beat in the egg a little by little. Add the flour, bicarb and baking powder and mix. When everything has combined, add the orange and lemon zest, add the mashed bananas, most of the walnuts (save a few for the top) and sprinkle in the vanilla essence. You will be left with a fragrant mixture with a lovely soft consistency.

Grease your loaf tin liberally. A tin that is roughly 8 x 20 x 10cm will be the right sort of size.

Spoon your banana cake mixture into the tin, and sprinkle the remaining walnuts over the top. Put on to the middle shelf of your oven and allow your Banana Loaf Cake to bake for 1 hour. It will turn a glossy rich brown colour. Pop in a clean knife or a skewer to check if it is done - if the knife comes out pretty clean then it is cooked.

Allow your banana bread to cool in its tin as it will collapse if you try to take it out too soon. When it is cool enough to handle - after 10 minutes or so - turn it out of its tin and carve up into delicious sweet and moist slabs.

Pour yourself a cup of nice tea and enjoy.

Mauritian Tea

Bois Chéri is the most famous of all Mauritian teas. It is grown in the Domaine de Bois Cherie which is a beautiful and lush tea plantation with views all the way down to the South coast of the Island.

If you would like to make tea the Mauritian way you will need:

- Milk - 1/2 cup per person
- Water 1/2 cup per person
- A couple of crushed cardamon pods
- A teaspoon of Bois Cherie Vanilla Tea
- Sugar to taste

Method:

Bring the milk, water and cardamon to the boil. Add the tea and allow it to infuse to your taste.

Strain, add sugar, stir well.

Gulab Jamun

Pronounced Goo-lab Ja-moon

Gulab jamun are universally adored cardamon flavoured cakes that are first fried then soaked in syrup. A few days before a Mauritian wedding huge quantities of these little beauties will be made - sometimes entire rooms will be filled with pots brimming with them.

This recipe will make around 34- 35 gulabs.

Ingredients:

- 1 can of condensed milk (when a recipe starts like this you know that you're going to end up with something tasty)
- 750 oz of self raising flour, sieved
- 1/2 teaspoonful of ground cardamon
- 2 tablespoonfuls of vegetable oil (not olive oil, sunflower oil is perfect for this)
- 3 cups of vegetable oil for frying

For the syrup you will need:

- 450ml of cold water
- 1 cup of sugar, either brown or white will work well

Method:

If you plan to serve these Gulabs in the afternoon, start to make the dough in the morning. Or you can make the dough the night before.

If you want to make your own ground cardamon it's a very simple process. All you need to do is to take 3 - 4 cardamon pods and toast them in a dry frying pan over a medium flame for about 2 minutes. Toasting them in this way makes them easier to grind. Once they are done grind them in your grinder, or in the pestle and mortar that is sitting decoratively on your kitchen windowsill. My dad grinds his in a coffee grinder. Grinding your own cardamon is worth it - the aroma really is lovely.

Add the self raising flour and your freshly ground cardamon to the mixing bowl. Drizzle 2 spoonfuls of oil over the flour and using your hands work the oil into the flour for a little while, a minute or so is all it will take.

Now, use a can opener to make 2 holes on opposite sides of the top of your tin of condensed milk. Using a knife widen the holes that you have made in the tin as this will help you to pour the condensed milk out faster.

Slowly pour your milk on top of the flour whilst mixing everything together either by hand or using a spoon. You are looking to make a soft dough, just the same consistency as a bread dough. It will be very sticky - we are talking about a can of condensed milk after all! Rubbing a little oil onto your hands will help you to unstick and will help you to produce a nice shiny ball of dough.

Now, wrap the dough up in clingfilm and set this aside in a cool place for 5 -6 hours or even overnight. If you choose to refrigerate it you'll need to remove it 1 hour before you plan to cook - if the dough is too cold it becomes unworkable.

Now, let's make the syrup.

In a largish pan, add your sugar to the cold water. Stir this well and heat over a medium flame. Keep stirring whilst it heats up and continue heating for roughly 5 minutes. Don't leave it alone, stir continuously so you can feel when it changes consistency. You will

DELICIOUS MAURITIUS   167

know when the syrup has cooked when it starts to thicken up and the consistency becomes sticky. Take the syrup off the heat and allow to cool.

Once your dough has had a chance to rest, pinch off small amounts and roll between your palms to create small sausage shapes around 2 1/2 inches long and about the width of 1 penny piece. Put the rolled sausage shapes onto a plate and repeat until you have made them all.

In a wok, warm up 3 cups of oil. Heat this over a medium flame until the oil starts to smoke slightly. One at a time, carefully lower your Gulab sausages into the oil, adding up to 6 at a time, and fry them until they are dark brown all over. Turn them over occasionally and make sure that they don't burn. They will puff up when they cook and turn into a bigger sized sausage. When they are a rich mahogany colour (deep brown but not ebony) remove from the hot oil using a slotted spoon and put onto a dry plate, one that is not lined with kitchen paper. Each batch of gulags will take around 5 minutes to fry. Repeat until you have finished cooking all of them in this way.

Now dip the Gulabs in the syrup and leave them there for a minute or so to allow them to absorb the delicious syrup. You may have to do this in batches to make sure that they all get a chance to take up enough syrup.

Store in a large bowl with a lid and allow your guests to help themselves.

Jilabi

Pronounced Gee-Lay-Bee

You can find these gorgeous orange squiggly cakes piled up high in Indian sweet shop windows - and now you can make them yourself at home for free. When you bite in to these crispy cakes they go pop and release a saffron tinged syrup.

According to my mum this recipe will make 34 Jilabis precisely

Ingredients:

- For the Jilabis
- 1 medium cup of plain flour
- 1 tablespoonful of Besan flour
- 1/4 teaspoonful of ground cardamon - home made (see the previous recipe) or ready ground also works fine
- 1 pinch of baking powder
- 1 pinch of bicarbonate of soda
- 3 tablespoonful of plain yoghurt
- Cold water - around 1/2 cup
- 3 cups of vegetable oil to fry

For the syrup:

- 1 cup of water
- 1 cup of caster sugar.
- Pinch of saffron

DELICIOUS MAURITIUS

You will also need to have a squeezy plastic bottle with a nozzle. An empty plastic ketchup bottle - the one that you squeeze, will be ideal. It goes without saying that you will need to clean this out thoroughly. Or you can use a piping bag. The nozzle hole at the top of the bottle needs to be about the size of a large nail. My mum started to describe how you could enlarge the hole to the correct size by heating up an actual nail and…at this point I might have taken a little siesta!

Method:

Mix everything bar the vegetable oil and the syrup mixture together in a mixing bowl making sure that you stir away any lumps. You're aiming to produce a lovely thickish batter - slightly thicker than a pancake mixture. Once you have produced this, set it aside for 1/2 hour to allow it to set slightly. If you want to plan ahead this batter can be left in the fridge and will be fine to use for up to 3 days.

It's now time to make your syrup. Add all of the ingredients together in a pan and heat this over a medium flame whilst stirring constantly. Heat this for about 4 - 5 minutes until the syrup starts to thicken and changes consistency. The saffron will have tinged everything a lovely yellow colour. Remove from the heat and keep this pan close to the cooker.

Now heat up your oil in a wok over a medium flame until the oil starts to smoke gently and is hot.

Fill up your empty ketchup / squeaky plastic bottle/ piping bag with the Jilabi batter. Starting with a dot in the middle squeeze out the Jilabi mixture in a squiggly fashion until you have made a squiggly round pattern of about 10 cm in diameter. You will be able to fit up to 5 of these shapes in the wok (depending on the size of your wok) Make sure that there are plenty of holes in your shape, don't fill them out. They are meant to have gaps throughout and it will be more crispy if you don't overfill. You are not looking to create a thick heavy biscuit, you are looking for a delicate scribble effect. Think Jackson Pollock rather than Beryl Cook.

Fry your squiggles on both sides until they have gone a pale golden colour. This takes barely any time, roughly 1 minute on each side, 2 minutes in total.

Remove the Jilabis from the hot oil using a slotted spoon and dunk this immediately into the syrup. Dunk it in and then take it out immediately. The Jilabi will soak up syrup with the greatest of ease, so don't leave them in for too long.

Remove the Jilabis from the syrup and put them onto a colander placed over a plate to allow excess syrup to be released. This excess syrup can be re used in the syrup pan.

To serve simply pile up your Jilabis on a pretty plate - a mini mountain of glossy orange happiness.

Besan Ludoo

Pronounced Bey-san Lud-ooh

Ganesh, the cheerful Hindu god with the pot belly and the elephant's head adores Ludoos. Something beloved by a god is bound to be a very good thing. Ludoos are a sort of round sweet that are slightly larger than a ping pong ball and much less bouncy. There are different types of Ludoos - they can be moist and sticky or dry and crumbly. This recipe is for the latter which happens to be my favourite sort. These ones have a sun kissed glow, the texture of hot baked sand and a toasted nut flavour and can last for several weeks in a sealed container. Just because they can does not mean that they will.

Note: Besan flour can be made out of either ground chickpeas or gram. My mum prefers to make them with ground gram. So if you want to cook like my Mauritian Mother look out for Gram Flour Besan in the Indian shop. It is a lovely soft yellow colour.

This recipe will make 8 Besan Ludoos.

Ingredients:

- 125 g of Besan flour (roughly 1 cup)
- 60 ml of melted butter (this starts off life as ½ a block of butter)
- 65 g of caster sugar (Mauritian Caster Sugar if you can get it as its the best!)
- 1/4 teaspoonful of ground cardamon
- 2 teaspoonfuls of ground almonds
- 2 teaspoonfuls of unsalted pistachio nuts, finely chopped

Method:

Put your wok on a low heat. Add the butter and allow this to melt. Next add your Besan flour to the melted butter and stir this in well. Keep stirring until the mixture turns a lovely golden colour. This will take around 10 minutes. Don't leave it alone at any point or it will stick and spoil.

Use a spatula to scoop the mixture out of the pan. It is important to do this as if you keep it in the pan it will keep on cooking, so empty it all out into a fresh bowl. Leave this to cool on the side for 15 - 20 minutes. Don't put it in the fridge.

When it's cool enough, add the ground almonds, cardamon and sugar to the Besan and butter mix and using a spoon stir everything together until it is all well combined.

Divide the mixture into 8 portions and then roll these into little ball shapes between your palms.

Put the rolled Besan ladoos onto a pretty plate and then sprinkle each one in the centre with a few of the chopped pistachio nuts.

Leave everything to cool down completely and then serve.

These can be refrigerated and stay good for a few weeks.

Gateau Batat

Pronounced Gat-oh Bat-tat

These are my all-time favourite Mauritian sweets.

A Gateau Batat is a soft and juicy sort of pie that is filled to brimming with freshly grated coconut. When you bite into it everything squishes and syrup oozes out. They are incredibly moist and very moreish. Batat is the Creole word for a sweet potato.

This recipe will make around 12 Gateau Batats.

Ingredients:

- 2 medium sweet potatoes. My mum cautions against getting the yellow fleshed varieties as these retain too much water. She suggests that you get the white fleshed ones instead - the ones with the mauve skins. Please do not peel them as they will absorb far too much water.
- 1/2 Fresh coconut. Desiccated coconut will not do as the resulting cake will be far too dry.
- 225g of plain flour - you may not need to use all of this
- 4 tablespoonfuls of granulated sugar
- 2 cups of vegetable oil to fry (corn oil is perfect)

Method:

Let us start off with the filling, it is very simple to make. First, finely grate the coconut. Sprinkle over 2 tablespoonfuls of sugar and mix together well. Set this aside.

We now need to prepare the sweet potatoes. This step is also easy as pie.

Add the unpeeled sweet potatoes to a large pan of boiling water and boil until they are soft. If you use a pressure cooker they will boil in around 5 minutes, if you use a normal pan, it will take up to 30 minutes. Check that they are cooked right through by piercing with a knife. When it is cooked the sweet potato will be soft - the consistency of a normal boiled potato. Remove the sweet potatoes from the water and allow these to cool.

Once they have cooled enough to handle, peel them and discard the skins which will slip off quite easily. Pop the peeled sweet potatoes into a bowl and mash them with a fork.

When the mashed sweet potatoes are completely cold, we need to start adding the flour. Add half of the flour first and using your hands start to bind the mixture together. You may not need to use all of the flour. You are trying to reach a stage where the mashed sweet potatoes transform into a workable soft dough. Stop adding the flour when you reach this point. The less flour at you are able to add the better as you will have a softer and more succulent cake that will melt in your mouth.

Dust your rolling pin and board with a little flour. Pick up all of your dough and try to roll this out in one go. This is so that you don't end up adding too much flour. Roll it out until your dough is about 3 mm thick (so it's actually quite thin)

Take out a round pastry cutter of around 8cm diameter and cut out as many shapes as you can out of your dough. Set these shapes aside on a big plate until you are ready to fill them. If your mixture is particularly sticky it is fine to add some flour to this plate so it doesn't stick.

Now it is time to assemble your Gateau Batats.

DELICIOUS MAURITIUS

Take one of your pastry circles and then add one tablespoonful of your coconut mixture to the middle of the circle. Fold the circle in half and create a D shape. Take a fork and gently press the prongs of the fork all around the open sides to press them together. This will ensure that your delicious mixture doesn't fall out when you are frying it. Think of a miniature Cornish pasty and this will give you the right idea.

Continue to fill up of your pastry circles until everything has been used up. If you run out of filling please don't fret: it wont take you long to grate some more coconut and stir in a bit more sugar.

Now it is time to fry your Gateau Batats.

Heat up your oil in a wok over a medium flame until it is smoking slightly.

Using a slotted spoon, lower the Gateau Batats into the oil one by one. Fry up to 4 of these at a time, turning them over occasionally. After about 2 minutes on each side they will turn a deep golden brown colour at which point they are done.

Remove from the oil and set onto a plate covered with a couple of sheets of kitchen paper to absorb any excess oil. Cook the rest of your batch until everything is done.

These marvellously squishy cakes can be eaten hot (careful - the sugar does melt when it is frying) or cold, when the sugary filling and pastry both remain soft and delightfully moist. Either are delicious.

Kheer

Pronounced Kir

This is often served at Mauritian weddings where it is, alongside the rest of the meal, served on a shiny green banana leaf. When I was little I was part of my cousin's wedding and had to eat a dollop of this tasty rice pudding as part of the ceremony. That would have been fine but I had no spoon. The calamity! Luckily someone noticed my distress and returned with a baby spoon and calm was restored.

This recipe will serve around 6 people as a lovely dessert. It is quite rich and is very good after a light vegetarian meal such as dal puri with aubergine curry. A left over dal puri goes very nicely with this creamy Kheer.

Ingredients:

- 1 cup of white basmati rice
- 1/2 cup of roughly chopped almonds. My mum prefers to keep the skin on as it's tastier that way
- 1/2 cup of sultanas
- 1 pint of milk
- 50 g of unsalted butter
- 1/4 cup of white granulated sugar
- 2 cardamons (or you can put 1/4 teaspoonful of ground cardamon instead)
- 1 teaspoonful of fennel seeds
- 2 cloves

Method:

Wash your rice throughly in a few changes of water. Then, drain this rice in a colander.

Put 2 cups of water to boil in a saucepan. Do not cover the pan. Add the rice and bring this to the boil over a high flame. Once the rice starts to bubble and boil reduce the heat to a low flame and allow to cook uncovered until the water has evaporated and the rice has cooked. If you cover it the rice will boil over and you will have a big mess to clean up!

Now add the rest of your ingredients and stir everything well until you have mixed them in thoroughly. Keep cooking this over a low flame for 10 - 15 minutes, stirring regularly. At this point the rice will absorb half the milk and have become lovely and creamy. When you reach this point put the lid on.

Cook the Kheer covered for the last 3 minutes, giving it a stir every minute until the rest of the milk has been absorbed into the rice. Turn off the heat. Give it a final stir, lick the spoon and keep covered until you are ready to eat.

Tukmaria

Pronounced Tuk-maar-ia

Tukmaria are tiny seeds that are otherwise known as Sweet Basil Seeds. Once soaked in water they swell up into little mauve pearls, forming the basis of a sweet and cooling drink that is adored by children and adults alike and sold by the barrow in Port Louis market.

In addition to the taste, I love Tukmaria because of its frogspawny looks and texture. If for some unknown reason you find the idea of drinking frogspawn off-putting, simply close your eyes and think of its modern Japanese counterpart, bubble tea.

This is very important: Prepare this drink in a jug that you can easily clean - a glass jug is perfect. I once made this in an antique copper kettle and the little seeds stuck to every single interior surface and clogged up its spout. It took forever to clean especially as it took over an hour for me to to pluck up the courage to plunge my hand into its amphibious depths...

This will make one jug of Tukmeria.

Ingredients:

- 3 tablespoonful of Tukmeria seeds (Indian shops will sell this and they are also available online)
- 1 jug of water
- 2 - 3 tablespoonfuls of sugar

DELICIOUS MAURITIUS

Method:

Mix everything together and stir until the sugar has dissolved. Leave for an hour or so until the seeds turn into tiny mauve balls. When you are ready to serve, swirl the mixture around and make sure that you distribute everything evenly. If you like, you can top up with some milk, or condensed milk if you're feeling so inclined.

It's very refreshing.

Poa

Pronounced Poe-ah

As their name suggests, Poas are sweet doughy clouds with chubby brown tummies. A diddle dumpling in cake form. My mum describes them as little doughnuts enriched with nuts, spices and sultanas. If you eat them super fresh from the wok the sultanas are warm and particularly succulent. This is a very simple cake to make and is perfect for tea time on Friday after school.

A Poa sets the weekend off in exactly the right sort of way.

This recipe will make 16

Ingredients:

- 1 cup (300g) of plain flour, you don't need to sieve it
- 2 tablespoonfuls of sugar
- 1 tablespoonful of vegetable oil (like corn oil)
- 3/4 cup of whole milk
- 2 tablespoonfuls of chopped almonds
- 2 tablespoonfuls of sultanas
- 1/4 teaspoonful bicarbonate of soda
- 1/4 teaspoonful of ground cardamon
- 1 teaspoonful of fennel seeds
- 2 cups of vegetable oil to fry

Method:

First you need to make a soft batter. In a bowl combine the flour, oil, sugar, bicarbonate and milk and stir this all together with a spoon.

DELICIOUS MAURITIUS

Now add all the rest of the ingredients and stir it all together well. Cover your bowl and leave this to set for 1/2 hour.

Now, heat up your oil in your wok. Heat this over a medium flame until the oil starts to smoke. Now, mix your batter up again to make sure all of the nuts etc are well distributed and take a tablespoonful of your batter mixture and spoon this directly into your hot oil. Repeat this in a separate part of the oil until you have used up your batter mixture (around 5 or 6 spoonfuls) and have a wok filled with cooking Poas - they will puff up in the hot oil. Turn these over after 2 minutes and allow to cook on the other side for another 2 minutes. They will go a deep golden brown colour when they are done.

Remove from the oil using a slotted spoon and allow the excess oil to drain away on a few sheets of kitchen paper.

Sit back, watch your programme, and enjoy with a nice cup of tea.

A variation: Banana Poa

To make this, simply mash up 2 ripe bananas and add this to the Poa batter mixture. You will only need 1 spoonful of sugar as the bananas provide the sweetness and 1/2 cup of milk, as the bananas provide ample sogginess! Cook in the same way. A Banana Poa is even more succulent than a regular one.

Tekwa

Pronounced Tay-Qua

Neither my mum or me knew how on earth to spell this. We both however know how to say it - and definitely know how to eat them! Tekwa is one of my nephew Maxi's favourite cakes. He can eat a pile of these in one go.

Tekwa is a round thick biscuit. Slightly thick, slightly chewy and very tasty indeed.

Ingredients:

- 1 cup of flour
- 2 tablespoonfuls of vegetable oil
- 1 pinch of bicarbonate of soda
- 2 tablespoonfuls of ground almonds
- 2 tablespoonfuls of milk powder
- 1/4 cup of sugar
- 1/2 cup of full cream milk
- 1/4 teaspoonful of ground cardamon seeds
- 1 teaspoonful of fennel seeds (optional, it does taste nice though so give it a try)
- 1 1/2 cups of oil for frying

Method:

Use your fingers to mix the flour, milk powder and oil together in your mixing bowl, and rub everything together nicely to create some light breadcrumbs.

Now add the sugar, cardamon, bicarb and fennel seeds. Work these through your breadcrumb mixture until everything is well distributed.

Create a well in the middle of your dry mixture. Pour half of your milk into the middle of this and mix everything together using a spoon. Add small quantities of the milk to this mixture little by little until your dough is the consistency of bread dough. It must not be too soggy or too stiff. According to my mum, you are aiming for a nice soft dough.

Now you need to knead this dough for 5 minutes. There is no need to flour the surface or your hands as the oil in the mixture will stop it from sticking. If you feel that it needs a little more encouragement, add a few drops of oil to your hands to help. Cover the nice soft dough and set it aside. You can put it into the fridge if you like but it is not necessary. Leave it to rest for 1/2 hour.

Once rested, pinch off small quantities of your dough. They need to be lightly smaller than a ping pong ball, and slightly bigger than that big marble that you won when you played marbles at school. Rub a tiny bit of oil onto your rolling board and put your dough into the middle of this. Roll it out into a circle of roughly 8cm diameter and 3 mm thick. They are quite thin but don't worry.

Heat up your oil now in a wok over a medium heat until it smokes slightly. Use your fingertips to lift up the rolled dough and add carefully to the hot oil. Allow this to cook for 2 1/2 minutes on each side turning it over with a slotted spoon. You will notice your Tekwa puffing up in the oil and it will turn into a lovely rich golden colour when it is ready.

Remove from the hot oil using your trusty slotted spoon and place on a plate covered in several sheets of kitchen paper to absorb excess oil.

Eat and enjoy.

Crunch!

Tekwa Dal

Pronounced Tay-qua Dal

This version of Tekwa is stuffed with a sweet dal filling. It is a little bit like the famous Dal puri, only much stockier. If you eat it when it is hot it will be lovely and soft, the sugar will melt and make friends with the dal and the coconut. Eat it at tea time or happily round up your dinner with one or two of these. This recipe will make 6 of these bountiful beauties.

Ingredients:

- For the dough
- 1/2 lb of plain flour, sieved
- 1 pinch of bicarbonate of soda
- 1 pinch of baking powder
- 14 tablespoonfuls of water or milk (or mix of bit of both)
- 2 tablespoonfuls of vegetable oil

For the filling:

- 1/2 cup of cooked channa dal
- 3 tablespoonfuls of caster sugar
- 1 teaspoonful of ground fennel seeds
- 1/4 teaspoonful of ground cardamon
- 2 tablespoonfuls of freshly grated coconut
- 2 cups of vegetable oil to fry

Method:

In a bowl, together the flour, bicarbonate of soda and baking powder. Drizzle over the oil and combine everything together until you have made nice crumbly breadcrumbs. Now add the water and knead this all together for about 8 minutes until you have a nice medium dough. Cover it - you don't want it to dry up - and set this dough aside. If you are making this the day before, stick it in the fridge and allow it to come back to room temperature before you use it. If you are lucky enough to have a nice container with a lid then stick it into that (my mum is overly proud of her recent purchase and asked me to add that bit in!)

On to the filling:

Grind up your cooked channa dal. You can use a heavy rolling pin to do this or you can use an electric or baby food grinder - just don't go too soggy, its good if it is ever so slightly rough. Now sprinkle over the sugar, fennel, cardamon and grated coconut and stir everything together well. It will smell so good - sweet, fresh and lightly spiced.

The return of the dough:

Divide your dough into six equal portions and roll them between your palms to make nice round balls. Poke your thumb into the ball and spoon in roughly a tablespoonful of your filling. Pull dough around the opening and seal the ball shut again.

Lightly flour your rolling pin and your board. Gently, now don't be heavy handed here, roll out your dough until it is roughly the size of a saucer. You can go smaller if you like, just don't roll it out too thinly or it might split when it comes to frying.

Heat the oil in a wok or frying pan over a medium flame. When the oil is hot, gently pick up the rolled out dough and put this into the

DELICIOUS MAURITIUS   187 hot oil making sure not to splash. Allow to fry for 1.5 minutes on each side. The cake will turn a golden yellow colour when it is done. Remove from the oil using a slotted spoon draining off excess oil and put onto a plate covered with several sheets of kitchen paper to soak up the rest.

Corn Pudding

Corn pudding!

I love corn pudding - A golden disc, a delightfully squidgy cake.

Ingredients:

- 1 cup of ground corn, either coarsely ground or smoothly ground. This is a pale yellow colour. You can buy ground corn from Indian supermarkets
- 2 cups of water
- 2 tablespoonfuls of granulated sugar
- 2 tablespoonfuls of sultanas
- 1 cup of whole milk
- 1 tablespoonful of butter
- 2 cardamon pods (or 1/4 spoonful of ground cardamon powder)
- 2 cloves
- 3 tablespoonfuls of freshly grated coconut. You can use desiccated, but freshly grated does taste so much nicer.
- 2 cups of water

Method:

Warm your butter in a pan over a medium flame until it melts slightly. This will take just a minute.

Add your water, sugar, sultanas, cardamon and cloves to the pan. Allow this to boil. This will take around 3-4 minutes.

DELICIOUS MAURITIUS

When your mixture is bubbling away merrily, add your corn, milk and 2 tablespoonfuls of your grated coconut. Stir this well and keep stirring. You will notice something miraculous happening, the moisture will start to thicken and take on a lovely custardy texture. Keep stirring. The mixture will keep thickening. You want to reach a thick consistency that is still just about possible to pour. This will take around 5 minutes in total. Make sure you keep stirring!

Lightly grease a dinner plate all over with a smidgin of butter. It's helpful if the plate has slight sides to it (to contain the pudding!)

Pour your corn pudding mixture into the centre of the plate until it fills it and is roughly 1/2 inch thick. Using a spatula, spread the mixture evenly. Now sprinkle the left over grated coconut all over the top of your corn pudding.

Leave the pudding to cool down uncovered for a couple of hours and then it will be ready to eat.

Just before serving, score the surface with a knife into 8 portions. (This is my mum's attempt to be fancy. I do not remember any such scores when I was little.) Use a knife to cut the pudding and have a saucer nearby to flop it into.

Eat with a fork whilst winding down at tea time.

About my Dad's Mother

My dad's mother lived in a tiny house under a corrugated roof right in the middle of a mountain. Every day she would walk up the mountain slopes and gather fresh fodder for the cow that lived in a shed round the back. When my dad would go back home to Mauritius on holiday she would march down from her mountain top to visit, stay with him for a couple of days and then walk herself back home. She was skinny dark and wrinkled as a root, and lived upright and healthy well into her 90s. All that walking clearly suited her.

In the end she had a stroke and wasn't able to walk any more. I visited her on her sick bed and she cried happy tears and offered me a banana and an orange. When she died they drove her by 4 x 4 deep into the heart of the mountain and laid her to rest in a circle of stones.

Napolitaines

Pronounced Na-poli-ten

Now this is not officially one of my mum's recipes. But it is certainly a very Mauritian cake which is sold in bakeries throughout the land. Napolitaines are soft, jam-filled biscuity confections that are topped with a smooth pink icing. Our name for them was Granny Cakes. Once you make them I think that you will agree that they do have a very grannyish look about them.

This recipe will make 12 granny cakes

Ingredients:

- 300g white plain flour
- 300g unsalted butter, softened
- Strawberry jam
- 300g icing sugar
- 2 tablespoonfuls of soya milk
- A couple of drops of pink food colouring

Method:

Preheat the oven to 180 or 160 fan

Mix the flour and butter together to make a dough.

Roll this out to 1cm thick.

Using a 9cm diameter cutter, cut out 24 circles from the rolled out dough.

Place on a non stick baking tray and bake for 15 minutes.

Once the cakes are cool enough to handle spread over a thin layer of jam, and sandwich two cakes together so that the jam remains on the inside. Place on a wire rack.

Now, make your icing.

Add 300g of icing sugar to 2 tablespoonfuls of soya milk and mix this together. You are looking for a slightly runny consistency that still allows you to see a figure of eight when you run a spoon through it. Add a few drops of food colouring and mix well.

Spoon this over your napolitaines until they are completely covered and let them dry for a few hours.

Eat wearing your bed jacket, slippers and half moon glasses.

Satwa

Pronounced Sut-wuh

According to my mum Satwa is full of flavour, goodness and nourishment. It made by grinding together lots of toasted dried nuts and seeds and then mixing this with a little milk into a gritty nutty paste. It is very tasty. A long time ago, if people made a pilgrimage to Grand Bassin - the holiest part of the island - or went to toil in the sugar cane fields all day long they would bring a little Satwa in a bowl to sustain them.

In Mauritius, the sister of your mother is known as your Mausi. Mausi was just lovely. She lived in the North of Mauritius by the seaside in a place called Grand Gaube. Mausi came to England once and taught my mum how to make this. It was very exciting seeing the various ingredients being measured out and toasted in turn. It was even better when I finally got to eat it mixed with milk and sprinkled with sugar or a spoonful of honey.

This recipe will make loads. Enough for plentiful servings. It will last for months in an airtight jar.

Ingredients:

This recipe will create a powder. All of the ingredients are therefore dry

- 1/4 lb of white basmati rice (or you could buy pre-popped rice, but where is the fun in that?) washed and left to dry out overnight until it is perfectly dry
- 2 tablespoonfuls of vegetable oil for the corn

- 1 teaspoonful of vegetable oil to cook the rice
- 1/4 lb of corn kernels (pop corn before the pop as it were)
- 1/4 lb of whole toasted channa (don't worry, it is sold in Indian shops. This is not channa dal)
- 1/4 lb of black or green lentils
- 1/4 lb of toasted unsalted peanuts
- 1/4 lb of unsalted toasted almonds, skin on or off. Don't worry if you can't find this as you can very simply toast them yourself.
- 1/4 lb of milk powder (this is optional, you can add this if you want to be able to just add water to your finished product)

Method:

Preheat your oven to low and allow to heat up.

Almonds and peanuts. Complete this step if your almonds and peanuts are raw, and not toasted. You can skip it if they are already toasted. Once the oven has preheated, put your almonds and peanuts onto a clean dry baking tray and leave then to toast for around 5 minutes then check on them every minute or so after that as they can so easily burn. You will know that the nuts have toasted properly as they will have a crunchy texture and won't have that raw flavour to them. They won't necessarily change colour, so you need to be on high nut alert! Once toasted, remove from the oven immediately and set aside to cool on a very dry plate.

Now on to the popcorn.

Put 2 tablespoonfuls of oil to warm in a large pan over a medium flame. When the oil heats up, add your corn kernels. Swoosh these around in the pan with a wooden spoon with a long handle. Have your lid nearby. Once the oil heats up the kernels will start to pop, transforming from bright yellow kernels to popcorn. Cover it all up

DELICIOUS MAURITIUS

and shake the pan whilst everything pops away merrily. Once the pops start to spread out about 1 pop a second or more, remove from the heat. You don't want to scorch things. Set the popcorn aside in a very dry bowl and allow to cool.

Now onto the rice. Popped rice!

Add one teaspoonful of oil to the pan and heat this again over a medium temperature. Now, add your dry rice to the pan and then stir this around in the oil. Amazingly the rice will start to puff up just as the popcorn does, and it will turn a lovely crispy texture with a pale golden colour to it. When it starts to pop and puff, turn the heat down to low. Again, be aware that you don't want to let anything burn, so keep stirring and shaking your pan. You don't need to put the lid on it - the rice explosions are not as dramatic as the popcorn. Set the rice aside in a super dry bowl.

Now we need to do the lentils:

Add a teaspoonful of oil to the pan and heat this over a medium temperature. Now add your lentils to this and toast it. Stir the lentils around. My mum has forgotten if these pop up!

The lentils won't transform in any dramatic way, so just toast it in the pan stirring regularly over. Medium flame for 10 minutes. After this point, try to crush the lentil with a spoon and it is crushes easily using a heavy rolling pin or a spoon, then it is done. Put into a, yes you guessed it, a very dry bowl.

Channa

Do not toast this, buy it ready toasted. You will be there all day otherwise. You just don't have enough time to toast channa. You can put your channa into a very dry bowl though so it doesn't feel left out.

Now comes the fun part.

Put all of the ingredients into your coffee grinder and grind it all until it is the texture of coffee coarse grounds. Mix all of the various good things together including the dry milk powder (if you want to use this) and stir it all together well. You will be left with a sandy, powdery mixture and this needs to be kept in an airtight completely dry jar.

To serve, add a couple of large tablespoonfuls of the powder to a small bowl and add some sugar to taste. Mix in some milk (or water, if you already added milk powder) until it is roughly the consistency of slightly runny and grainy ice cream.

DELICIOUS MAURITIUS

A Reflection on Mauritian Picnics

A traditional Mauritian picnic requires extensive planning. Several families will need to be informed in advance and a small coach may need to be hired.

You will visit a few Mauritian beauty spots - Rochester Falls is an idyllic freezing cold waterfall with a basin lined with smooth basalt boulders. Bain Boeuf is a sweet rocky beach - I think it gets its name because the boulders in the sea look like the backs of bathing cows. Chamarel is a mystical place with shifting sands in rainbow hues. My sister Benny has memories of scampering over those multicoloured dusty dunes when she was little.

A Mauritian picnic menu doesn't generally involve sandwiches and crisps. Instead you can expect stacks of dal purees, an octopus salad, tandooried chicken and fish. At each beauty spot stop we'll eat a little more. Fingers and plates get rinsed in the sea and then its back on board the coach and on to the next destination.

Cornettos in the car

One of my fondest food memories was made outside Hampton Court. We had planned a day of sightseeing and picnicking and frolicking in the maze, only for all of our plans to be swept aside by torrential rain. All was not lost. We ate our picnic in the car, mum and dad in front, us four squeezed tight in the back, and my dad ran out to get us Cornettos.

It was a happy day.

La Laura

La Laura (pronounced la-lo-ra, say it quickly, roll the r in the back of your throat) is where my dad's parents lived, where he was brought up and from where he departed at the tender age of 25 to make his fortune in London where all the streets are paved with gold.

Tourists who are interested in exploring further than the fine Mauritian coastline or indeed the fringes of their lovely beach towel are well advised to visit La Laura. I remember my mum telling me that when she got married her friends were surprised that it didn't appear to have electric lights and that gibbons possibly hid in that misty green vegetation.

Imagine a mountain covered in a hundred different shades and textures of green. The perilously balanced boulder atop Peter Both mountain surrounded by sugar cane speckled with chickens and lonely goats all punctuated by an occasional moo. The tang of wood smoke and cooking sizzles gently mingling and drifting upwards. A sparkling river shivering blackly along an ancient volcanic trail. La Laura is a place of breathtaking natural beauty.

And so when my parents brought their inner city born South London raised children with them to pay their first visit to this blessed scene of course we kicked up a stink. I remember my sister Benny whispering urgently "Don't drink it. It's not pasteurised" when I was handed a glass of milk. She was right, it wasn't pasteurised. My grandparents had milked the cow that afternoon.

Semolina balls

Pronounced Sem-o-leena balls

This will make 12 balls

Ingredients:

- 150g of coarse or smooth semolina
- 25g of butter
- 1/4 teaspoonful of ground cardamon powder
- 2 tablespoonfuls of chopped almonds
- 2 tablespoonfuls of sugar
- 2 cloves
- 2 tablespoonfuls of sultanas
- 2 tablespoonfuls of desiccated coconut
- 1 teaspoonful of fennel seeds
- 500ml of milk

Method:

Our pudding starts with a dry heavy bottomed pan. Toast your semolina in this over a medium flame until it changes colour from a light beige colour to a lovely golden brown. This will take roughly 5 minutes and you will need to keep stirring your semolina continuously whilst it gets its suntan.

Remove the toasted semolina from the pan and set aside. Now add the butter and toss it around in the still warm pan and let it melt. You do not need to heat your pan at all for this part. Once it has melted slightly for a few seconds, add the cardamon, coconut,

DELICIOUS MAURITIUS

201

almonds, sugar, cloves, sultanas and fennel. Mix everything together.

Now add the milk, stir and allow to boil over a medium flame. This will take a few minutes.

When the milk comes to the boil add your semolina slowly, lower the heat to low and stir everything quickly. This will help to prevent your semolina from developing lumps. When the semolina has absorbed all of the milk it will have a silky smooth consistency and is ready to enjoy.

You can either eat the semolina as it is which is delicious served in a bowl with a spoon. Or you can wait until it is slightly cooler and fashion it into ping pong size balls and then roll in desiccated coconut.

Some Common Mauritian Phrases

Ke mo pou faire ek sa chilli coco?
What am I meant to do with this coconut chutney?

Anou manger, boire, amuser
Lets enjoy ourselves

Senti un peu malade
I feel a bit unwell

Kee toooe pou faire?
What are you doing?

En chi-gin de la sauce
A little bit more sauce

En chip chi boot
A little bit

Assez! Assez!
Enough!

Urre?
Huh?

Toe pe cose creole?
You speak creole?

Mo pa pe cose creole
I don't speak creole

Say tro Chaud
Its too hot

Encore Schou Schou?
Do you want more Schou Schou?

Vegetables and Vegetarian Food

- Schou Schou
- A Vegetarian Feast: Pumpkin, Kutchoo, Cabbage and Channa Dal
- Butterbeans in Light Tomato Broth
- Butterbean Curry
- Spicy Chickpeas
- Bean Curry
- Egg curry
- Easy Cook Ladies Fingers
- Cauliflower, Potato and Pea Curry

Schou Schou

Pronounced Soo-soo

Schou schou are pale green vegetables. They look like slightly transparent slightly anaemic pears. They have a very light taste (some might say bland) reminiscent of marrow, but it fills your stomach and is good for those that are on a diet. They have tiny prickles on the outside.

This dish goes well with tomato chutney, cabbage, channa dal, a pickle of some sort and a nice hot faratha or two. When I was last there my uncle plucked a schou schou from the road by his house. They grow quite happily in the Mauritian climate.

So beloved is this vegetable that there is even a Mauritian song called "Encore Schou Schou" (Translated as More Schou Schou)

This recipe serves 4 people as a side dish.

Ingredients:

- 1 lb of schou schou (this is roughly 2 of them. They are fairly dense and weigh a lot)
- 1/4 of an onion, finely chopped
- 1 clove of garlic
- Salt to taste
- 1 tablespoonful of vegetable oil
- 3 tablespoonfuls of water

Method:

Peel the schou schous and slice into halves. Remove the seeds. Slice it into 1 cm slices lengthways.

Rince your peeled slices now under running water.

Heat your oil in a small pan over a medium heat. Add the onion and allow to soften for a minute or so, stirring occasionally. Don't let it get too brown as this is a light dish. Now add the schou schou, garlic salt and water and stir this gently. Lower the heat to low, cover, and allow to simmer for about 10 minutes.

Take a peek, if you can see water, remove the lid and allow to cook for another few minutes. You can tell that it is cooked when press the schou schou with a fork it is very soft, like a well cooked marrow.

Remove from the heat and serve immediately.

A Vegetarian Feast: Pumpkin, Kutchoo and Channa Dal

This combination of food is perfect to tuck into at the end of a pious day. The bright orange sweet Pumpkin goes so well with an oil slicked Puri and the savoury tang of the Kutchoo.

Pumpkin

Ingredients:

- 1 lb of fresh pumpkin, peeled and chopped into chunks
- 1 clove of garlic, peeled crushed and chopped
- 1/4 onion, finely chopped
- 1 tablespoonful of vegetable oil
- 3 tablespoonfuls of water
- 1/2 teaspoonful of caster sugar (optional)
- Sprinkle of chopped coriander for garnish

Method:

Put your oil into your cooking pan to heat over a medium flame. When the oil has heated up, add your onion and allow this to fry for 30 seconds or so just so that it softened slightly.

Add the pumpkin and garlic now and stir everything together. Add the water now and lower the heat to low, cover the pan and allow to simmer. Allow this to gently cook for five minutes. Take a look and try to mash the pumpkin to see if it is soft. If it squashes very easily then it is cooked. If its a bit tough then simmer again for another 5 minutes and add a splash or two more water to prevent it from sticking. The length of cooking time depends on how old and tough your pumpkin is. Young ones are more tender and take less time to cook.

Once your pumpkin is nice and soft, you can mash it up using a fork or a potato masher. It will be a glistening orange colour. Taste it. If it tastes sweet enough don't add the sugar. If your pumpkin is in need of a bit of sugar, give it a sprinkle. It will be bright orange and slick with nutrients moist and glistening.

Pop into your serving dish and strew artfully with your chopped coriander.

Kutchu

Kutchu. How do you pronounce Kutchu? Imagine that you have a sneeze and add a K in front....Katchu!

It is a well known plant in India and in Mauritius that grows in the water and close to rivers. It is sold in bunches of tall mauve stalks with long green leaves. A little bit like young spinach, when you cook Kutchu it becomes a comforting deep green mush that tastes of vitamins and a strong tang of iron. You need to add lots of spices to this dish or the flavour of the leaves on its own will be too overpowering.

Ingredients:

- 1 lb of Kutchu, washed and finely chopped. Use both the stalk and the leaves.
- 1 medium onion, finely chopped
- 3 cloves of garlic
- 2 tablespoonfuls of oil
- 3 tomatoes, chopped (or you could use ½ a tin of tomatoes if you prefer)
- A few sprigs of thyme
- 1 teaspoonful of salt
- 1 inch cube of ginger, peeled and finely grated

DELICIOUS MAURITIUS

Method:

Set your cooking pot to heat over a medium flame. Add the oil and allow to heat. When the oil is hot, first add your onion and stir this for a minute until the onion starts to soften.

Now add the Kutchu, garlic and ginger, sprinkle with salt and stir this well. Lower the heat to low, cover and simmer and allow to cook for 10 minutes. Add your tomatoes and thyme now and allow to simmer again, stirring occasionally for another 10 minutes. If at any point it looks like things are sticking splash in some water and stir around.

Your Kutchu will be cooked when everything has softened and blended together. It will have a soggy spinach consistency.

Remove from heat and serve.

Simple Cabbage

This way of cooking cabbage is very clean and light. It tastes slightly sweet. The addition of the potato is a nice touch and enriches it. I like to eat this alone with faratha, although it is also a welcome component of your vegetarian banquet. It also goes well alongside a chicken or Lamb curry. You could make this with a green cabbage but I prefer the taste you get with a white one.

This recipe will serve 4 people as a side dish

Ingredients:

- 1 white cabbage (around 1lb) shredded into 1/2 cm widths
- 1 large potato
- 1/2 onion, chopped finely
- 1 clove of garlic, crushed and chopped
- 2 tablespoonfuls of oil
- 1 tomato, chopped
- 1 teaspoonful of salt
- 1 teaspoonful of mustard seeds

Method:

In large heavy bottomed pan heat up your oil over a medium flame. When the oil is hot, add your mustard seeds and stir them around. Immediately add the onion and potato and fry these together for a minute or so until the onions have turned slightly brown.

Add the cabbage, garlic and salt now and stir this to ensure that everything has mixed throughly and the oil has coated everything.

DELICIOUS MAURITIUS

Lower the heat to low, cover and cook for 10 minutes. If your cabbage is on the old side and is looking a bit dry, add a splash of water to prevent burning.

Next, stir everything well and add the chopped tomato and stir again. Cover it again and let it cook for another 5 minutes when everything will have cooked nicely.

Butterbeans in Light Tomato Broth

This is a very light way to eat butterbeans served in a light, tangy soupy base. It is lovely to eat this with some plain rice or a faratha to mop up the delicious juices.

This recipe will serve 4 people

Ingredients:

- 1/2 onion, chopped finely
- 1/2 lb of dried butterbeans, soaked in water overnight
- 2 cloves of garlic, chopped
- 1 sprig of thyme
- 2 tomatoes, chopped
- 1 pint of water
- 1 teaspoonful of salt
- 2 tablespoonfuls of vegetable oil
- 1/2 inch cube of ginger, grated

Method:

Let's start by draining away the water that your butterbeans have been soaking in. Add them to your pressure cooker together with the water and salt and allow this to cook on high under pressure. When your pressure cooker has whistled twice, reduce the heat to low and allow to boil for a further 5 minutes. Remove from the heat. As soon as you are able to, check that the beans have cooked. They

DELICIOUS MAURITIUS

will have a soft, floury texture when you press them between your fingers. If they are not cooked, let them boil for another 5 minutes or so. If you don't have a pressure cooker it will take a very long time to cook them and use too much gas! Leave the beans to wallow in their cooking liquor.

In a separate frying pan, now warm your oil over a medium heat. When it is hot, add your chopped onion and fry this until is has taken on a golden colour. This will take a couple of minutes. Next add the crushed garlic, ginger, thyme and tomatoes and stir these around. Lower the heat to low and cook this tomato mixture until everything had softened, and has cooked - it will be a lovely pink colour and the tomatoes will have broken down.

When this tomato sauce has cooked, scoop this out of the pan and stir it into your cooked butterbeans. At this point your mixture needs to be swimming in at least 1 cup of liquid. If its looking all a bit too dry, then add a splash more water.

Cover and let everything simmer together for 5 minutes. Dinner is served.

Butterbean Curry

This is a very popular curry in Mauritius. If you visit Port Louis Market you will certainly be offered this as a filling for your dal puri. This is a very spicy version and it has a slightly thick consistency.

Ingredients:

- 1 smallish onion, chopped
- 3 cloves garlic, chopped and crushed
- 1 teaspoonful of turmeric power
- 1 tablespoonful of curry powder - either mild, medium or hot. It's up to you.
- 2 tablespoonfuls of oil
- 1 teaspoonful of salt
- 1 inch cube of ginger, peeled and grated finely
- Small bunch of curry leaves (if you have them)
- 2 tomatoes, chopped
- 2 long aubergines, chopped into 1 inch cubes
- ½ bunch of chopped coriander
- ½ cup of water

Method:

Prepare your butterbeans as in the previous recipe. Once they are cooked, leave them in their cooking liquid to cool.

Cut up your aubergines, and wash in a colander. Put these aside.

In your cooking pot, put your oil to heat under a medium flame. When hot, add your chopped onion. Stir this around. When the

DELICIOUS MAURITIUS   217

onion has browned slightly - around a minute or so, add the turmeric and curry powder. Stir this around. Now add the water, ginger and garlic. Stir this again and let it cook for 2 minutes.

Now add your aubergine and the curry leaves. Cover up the pan, reduce the heat and allow to simmer for 5 minutes.

Now add the chopped tomatoes, stir well and allow to simmer for a further 5 minutes. When the aubergine is done, pour in the cooked butterbeans together with their cooking liquid, add the chopped coriander and allow this all to simmer over low heat for approximately 5 minutes until all the beans have heated through, swimming in a lovely rich ochre-hued sauce.

It is best served with dal puri, with plain boiled rice or it makes a lovely side dish for other curries.

Spicy Chickpeas

This is a simple and deliciously saucy side dish. Eat with rice or a nice hot naan and a spoonful of some sort of curry.

This recipe will serve 4 people.

Ingredients:

- 1 cup of dried chickpeas (½ lb)
- 1 teaspoonful of salt
- 1 small onion, chopped finely
- 2 cloves of garlic, crushed and chopped
- ½ inch cube of ginger, peeled and grated finely
- 2 tomatoes finely diced
- 1/4 bunch of coriander, washed and finely chopped
- 2 tablespoonfuls of Channa Masala powder (ask in an Indian shop. This is a complex mix of the following powders - coriander, chilli, pomegranite, black pepper, turmeric, cardamon, star anise, fennel cinnamon ginger, garlic, onion… It's better to get it ready made, you'll be there forever you try to make this yourself)
- ½ litre of water
- 2 tablespoonfuls of vegetable oil

Method:

Soak your chickpeas overnight in a pan of water

The next day, drain away the soaking water from the chickpeas. Add them to your pressure cooker together with the water and salt and

DELICIOUS MAURITIUS 219

allow this to boil under pressure for 5 minutes After this time, check to see if they have cooked. If they still feel a bit hard, boil them again for another 5 minutes or so. When they are cooked, the chickpeas will have a nice soft floury texture. Remove the cooked chickpeas from the pan in their cooking liquid and set aside.

Set a pan over a medium flame now and add the oil to heat. Once hot, add the onion and allow this to cook until it is golden. At this point add the channa masala powder and stir around for a minute.

Now add your tomatoes, the chickpeas together with their cooking liquid to the onion mixture and stir this around well. Lower the heat now to a low setting, cover and allow to simmer for 10 minutes. The channa masala mixture will thicken the sauce and it will have a spicy aroma.

Your chickpea curry will now be ready to eat. Simply strew with the coriander leaves as a final flamboyant gesture.

Bean Curry

This is my sister Meera's favourite food in the whole wide world - she absolutely adores bean curry! My mum would cook this for dinner every single Monday (we would always have vegetarian food on Mondays) and Meera would gobble up first one one, then two, then three plates of bean curry - each one served with a soft Faratha and a splash or two of Tomato Chutney.

If you can imagine a saucier, Indian version of chilli con carne - without the carne - you'll be in the right sort of area.

This recipe will feed 4-5 people, or if Meera is coming for dinner, maybe 2 people.

Ingredients:

- 1 cup of kidney beans. If you are using dry kidney beans, you will need to soak these overnight
- 1 medium onion
- 3 cloves of garlic
- 1 inch cube of ginger, peeled
- A few sprigs of coriander
- ½ a can of tinned tomatoes, or 2 - 3 fresh tomatoes
- 1 Aubergine chopped into 1 inch cubes
- Salt to taste
- 2 tablespoonfuls of curry powder
- 1 tablespoonful of turmeric powder
- Water
- 2 tablespoonfuls of vegetable oil

DELICIOUS MAURITIUS

Method:

Add a teaspoonful of salt to 3 medium cups of water. Add the drained kidney beans to this and bring this to the boil over a high flame. If you use a pressure cooker this will take about 10 minutes.

At this point you need to lower the temperature to a low flame and let it cook under pressure for another 10 minutes. After this time, turn the gas off and wait for the steam to leave the pan. Check to make sure that the beans are cooked. They will be cooked when the beans look dark brown (the water will be the same colour as well). The texture will be soft to the touch and the kidney beans will be easy to crush between your fingers (try not not let them go too mushy though) set the kidney beans and its cooking water aside.

Now finely chop up your onions and garlic and finely grate the ginger.

Heat up 2 tablespoonfuls of oil in a little frying pan over a medium flame, then fry the onion for a couple of minutes until they have gone golden brown in colour and have softened slightly. Add your curry powder, turmeric and garlic and ginger and tomatoes and stir. Add 3 tablespoonfuls of water to ensure that it doesn't burn or stick. Lower the heat and allow this sauce to cook gently for 5 minutes, stirring occasionally.

Next add the aubergine to the curry sauce, pop the lid back on and and cook under a low heat until the aubergine is tender. This won't take long - maybe 5 or 6 minutes - and you should stir things from time to time. Add some salt to taste.

It is now time to add your curry mixture to the cooked kidney beans. If there is more than a cupful of kidney bean liquid swilling around your pan discard some as you don't want it to be too watery. Mix everything together and cook on a low flame for around 5 minutes until everything is warmed through.

The bean curry is now ready to eat. You might like to have it with a simple tomato chutney. Plain boiled rice also goes well. It's nice to eat any leftovers with a plain omelette.

If Meera comes for dinner there probably won't be any leftovers.

The Blue Ford

My dad once arranged for a sky blue Ford car to be shipped back to Mauritius, a gift for his brothers.

A few years later on holiday back home he was astonished to discover that the car had been converted into a Chicken Coop. A very contented family of wide eyed chickens now counted that motor car as their primary residence.

What a comfortable coop that must have been for them - I imagine that they must have laid very big big eggs.

Egg Curry

This curry is perfect to whip up after work as it barely takes any time at all to prepare. I think that the eggs look like little curried aliens bobbing around in the sauce. This economical yet flavoursome recipe serves two.

Ingredients:

- 4 eggs
- 1 spoonful of curry powder
- 1 spoonful of turmeric
- 1 small onion, chopped
- 2 cloves of garlic
- 1 small cube of ginger
- 2 tomatoes
- A sprig of chopped dhania (or coriander to those that don't speak Creole)

Method:

Boil the eggs for 10 minutes. Shell them. Leave them aside.

In a small pan, fry the onion until they are a bit soft and a light brown colour. This will take less than 4 minutes.

Now add the curry powder and turmeric and allow this to fry together briefly.

Now, before things start to stick, add the tomato, garlic and ginger. Let this soften nicely under a medium flame. This will take 5 minutes.

Add 1/2 cup of water and stir this so that you have a nice sauce. Bring this to the boil and let it simmer for 5 minutes.

In the meantime take one of the boiled egg in one hand. In your other hand a small sharp knife. Gently score into the eggs - careful, you don't want to cut the eggs in two, you simply want the eggs to able to absorb a little of the sauce.

Once the curry sauce has simmered add the scored eggs. Stir it around gently so that the eggs are covered in the sauce and allow to cook on a very low heat for the final five minutes.

The eggs will soak up the sauce and they will turn a bright yellow.

Sprinkle with the chopped coriander and gobble up with rice and perhaps a fresh tomato salad on the side.

Easy Cook Ladies Fingers

Firstly, which lady has fingers that look like this? Ladies fingers are known as La Lo in Mauritius. When I discovered this I immediately took against them. Even to this day I feel a twinge of unhappiness when presented with a plate of them. If I had known that in England ladies fingers are known as okra I might have been able to palate them with more graciousness. This version makes for a quick and simple side dish.

Ingredients:

- 1 lb of ladies fingers
- 1/4 of an onion, finely chopped
- 1 clove of garlic
- 1 teaspoonful of salt
- 2 tablespoonfuls of oil

Method:

How to prepare your ladies fingers for cooking:

1) Wash your ladies fingers.
2) Now chop off the top and tail of your lady's fingers. This sounds a bit brutal doesn't it?
3) Slice 'em into 1 inch lengths (so you can hide them easily amongst nicer sounding vegetables)

DELICIOUS MAURITIUS

Warm your oil in a frying pan. When it is hot, add the onion and garlic and stir this around for a minute or two. Now add the chopped up fingers and add your salt. Reduce the flame to low, cover and allow to cook for 10 minutes, stirring occasionally. If it looks like things are sticking or if you are in a rush to eat your ladies fingers then add a few spoonfuls of water as this will speed up the cooking process. If you really can't wait put them in the pressure cooker!

Right before serving, turn up the heat and allow the water to evaporate and for the fingers to take on a slightly fired texture which even I admit is rather nice.

Try as an alternative to green beans. Eat it with rice, dal and maybe a nice salad on the side. Just don't call them La Lo and all will be fine.

Cauliflower, Potato and Pea Curry

This is so simple but utterly delicious. Very wholesome and filling. The vegetables cook in their own steam.

This will serve 4 people as a main course

Ingredients:

- 1 cauliflower, cut into florets
- 1 small onion, chopped
- 1 cube of ginger, grated finely
- 3 cloves of garlic grated or finely chopped
- 2 tomatoes
- ½ cup of frozen peas
- 2 potatoes, diced
- 1 tablespoonful of curry powder
- 3 tablespoonfuls of vegetable oil
- 1 teaspoonful of salt
- 1 teaspoonful of turmeric powder
- 1 pint of water
- A few sprigs of coriander, chopped

Method:

Put 1 pint of water to boil in a pan. When boiling add your cauliflower and boil this for one minute. Remove and drain and set aside.

In a medium-sized heavy-bottomed pan add the oil to heat over a medium flame. When hot, add the onions and allow to fry for minute until they soften slightly. Add the potatoes and allow these to fry for a minute, stirring occasionally.

Next add the cauliflower, garlic, ginger and salt. Stir gently for a minute and lower the heat slightly.

Now add the tomatoes, curry and turmeric powder. Stir thoroughly and make sure everything is coated well. Reduce the heat even more, cover (it will cook in its own steam) and allow to bubble away for about 10 minutes. Give it a quick stir every few minutes or so.

After 10 minutes add the peas, mix them in, cover and reduce the heat again to the lowest of the low. Check every few minutes to make sure that it is not sticking. If it does, add a little water.

When you are ready to eat, sprinkle the dish with your chopped coriander when you are ready to eat.

You can serve this gorgeous vegetarian meal with some dal and plain boiled rice. Your constitution will thank you for such an early digestible meal.

More sauce please:

If you want to have a slightly more saucy dish, add ½ cup of water when you add the tomatoes, curry and turmeric powder.

Dodo

Did you know that Mauritian mothers all over the world whisper the same word to soothe their babies to sleep?

"Dodo, Dodo" they say, accompanied with a gently consoling pat on the back.

Isn't it lovely that after all this time we still remember

About the Authors

Sonia Kawalputtee Durjun was born in Mauritius and lives in London where she successfully raised her children.

Kevin Durjun was born, raised and lives in South London. He is a practitioner of Chinese Medicine and broadcasts on health matters.

Printed in Great Britain
by Amazon